The Intersection of Joy and Money

What others are saying about Mackey McNeill!

This book will help everyone create and enjoy their personal wealth!

Jennifer Read Hawthorne, Co-Author
Chicken Soup for the Woman's Soul

A must read for anyone who wants to create and enjoy wealth.

Dr. Ivan Misner, Co-Author
Masters of Networking and Founder of BNI

Using the understandings from the Enneagram, Mackey brings insight and thoughtfulness to our relationship with money.

Dr. David Daniels, Co-founder
Enneagram Professional Training Program
in the Narrative Tradition.

Mackey McNeill brings new understanding and energy to our internal conversation around money, helping us to clear self-defeating thoughts, feelings, and behaviors.

Edwene Gaines
Unity Minister

[Mackey] made me think...and delivered me right to the core issues around how I use my money...I want more from Mackey McNeill!

Paul Shafer
Wisdom Television
and Radio Network

In the short time I have engaged [this] process, my life has transformed beyond what I could have imagined...and...my bank accounts are all off the charts! Mackey McNeill is pure Magic!

Lucy Morris, President
Phoenix Possibilities, Inc.

I love [Mackey's] presentation style; funny, caring, heartfelt and intelligent, what a combination!

Lee Myers, Chairman of the Board
New Thought Unity Center, Cincinnati

Mackey is an inspiration!

Max Gaenslen
Principa Client Service Manager

Mackey is truly in touch with her clients…

Steve Stravolo, CPA

I …struggled for years trying to determine why I handled money the way I did.
Mackey… gave me the answer.

Wayne Burchwell, Writer

In no time Mackey will be on Oprah!

Sarah Mohr

Mackey is magnetic.

Shannon Buzzanca

I'm betting [Mackey] will lead us to the promised land.

Charlie Jones

Working with Mackey, I saw I could manage my debt, begin saving, start a new career
and go back to school!

Monica Baltz

I highly recommend that anyone looking for focus and direction in their career consider
working with Mackey McNeill. My income jumped 70% in the first year while working
with Mackey .

Diane Samsel

…I learned that I must be conscious about my money life and responsible for my money
choices!!! Powerful…!!!

Nancy Steward

The Intersection of Joy and Money

A Workbook for Changing Your Relationship With Money

by Mackey Miriam McNeill, CPA/PFS

PROSPERITY
PUBLISHING

PROSPERITY
PUBLISHING

1881 Dixie Highway
Ft. Wright KY 41011
www.prosperitypublishing.com

Published by arrangement with Prosperity Publishing

Cover Design: Doris Jeffers with Lisa Ballard
Illustration: Lisa Ballard
Interior Design: Doris Jeffers
Cover Photography: David A. Ziser

For further information, contact Prosperity Publishing.

Library of Congress Catalog Control Number: 2002112272

ISBN: 0-9723563-0-4

First Printing November 2002

Prosperity Publishing and *The Intersection of Joy and Money* are registered trademarks of Prosperity Publishing.

Printed in USA

My life is divinely guided. Whatever my needs in accordance with my highest good, Universal Spirit provides. Becoming the author of this book required the courage to risk, to find faith in my own inner knowing. Two beautiful women appeared in my life with graceful synchronicity, helping me heal old wounds and find again the perfection of being human.

For Lucy Morris

who gave me her heart and taught me
to live in the moment

For Deb Ooten

who grounded me, loved me, and taught me
the power of being who I really am.

Table of Contents

Acknowledgements

Life is collaboration.

As we move from the fantasy that we are to be rugged individuals in the world, to a new reality of creating loving partnership with fellow human beings, life opens up to new possibilities. This book is one such possibility. Created with support from many people, it is a true creation of my community.

I gratefully acknowledge those communities and people who blessed me with their talent and leadership in the project.

To **Aunt Hickie** for her unending love and constant stand for my success and for sharing with me at a young age her wisdom of money magic.

To **Women Writing for (a) Change** for providing a venue for the first listening of this material.

To **Kathy Wade** for her gracious and superb editing, and for her initial feedback, *It's a real book!*

To **Doris Jeffers** for her design talents and for being a contributor of positive energy.

To the team at **Mackey McNeill Mohr, PSC**, for taking care of the details of business so I could focus on this material.

To divine guidance for bringing me the resources I needed just when I needed them.

To **New Thought Unity Center of Cincinnati**, and to **Doris Hoskins** and **Pat Williamson** for their inspiration.

To **Paul Coulter** for his wisdom, *Write and speak from your heart.*

To **my clients** who allowed me to practice these ideas.

To those individuals in my initial Cliff-jumping community: **Adaire Hiestand**, **Jack Armstrong**, **Kathie Martin Ossege**, and **Lisa James**, who became my dear friends and cheerleaders.

To **Roy and Bev Cardell** for the beautiful words, *We will always love you.*

To **Debbie Davis** for her enthusiasm, and for her divine synchronicity.

To **Sarah Mohr** for her love and encouragement.

Introduction

It is up to each of us to contribute something to this wonderful world.

— Eve Arden

The purpose of this book is to bring personal power to your relationship to money and to create self-defined prosperity. Whatever your money life looks like at present, this workbook provides the tools to transform it into one of joy.

This is not a technical *how-to* book. It will not answer all your questions on financial planning. There are plenty of books already written on the how-to's, including how to invest, how to buy insurance, how to buy real estate, etc.

Because your money life has many facets, we will touch on all of them, offering tips, advice and ways to learn more in each area.

Completing this book gives you the foundation to complete your own financial plan. There are a variety of resources available to you. Those resources include the Internet, the library, bookstores, classes at local universities and schools, and/or professional financial planning expertise.

Regardless of what resources you ultimately use to complete the technical components of your plan, the efforts you put into this workbook are critical to getting the results you truly desire. This workbook is a journey of self-discovery — the only beginning point for manifesting dreams.

Presently you may think of money as something out there, not a part of yourself. But money is a part of you. Your actions with money, such as receiving, spending, or investing, require alignment with your personal value system. As long as you treat your actions around money as separate from who you really are, you will not be in joy with money.

> *This workbook is a journey of self-discovery — the only beginning point for manifesting dreams.*

You are in joy when you express your unique self without fear of judgment in the world. If you are concerned about the environment, you take action to express this concern in the world. Perhaps you recycle, use environmentally friendly cleaning products, or avoid the use of chemicals on your lawn. But if you then invest in companies that indiscriminately pollute the environment, you are taking action with your money that is inconsistent with who you really are.

Why would you do such a thing? Out of fear. You cling to your money as if there were security in your investments. You are happy as long as your investments are increasing in value. When things go awry, and the market goes down in value, you look at the Enron, Tyco and WorldComs of the world and say, *They are to blame.* Yes, these companies got caught up in their own greed. In the process, many people got hurt. But if you were investing without concern for your personal values, only for profit, were you not participating in this same greed energy?

Now is the time for you to take responsibility for your money life and to stop blaming anything outside yourself for your unfulfilled desires. As you transform your relationship to money, many other facets of your life will shift.

Your way of being with money is a mirror for you to see yourself in the world. Use this workbook to bring into focus the image in your mirror, then alter the image to your own personal creation using the tool of conscious choice.

Change your relationship to money. Facilitate your own healing. Enjoy the journey. ∎

> *You are in joy when you express your unique self without fear of judgment in the world.*

1
My Own
Journey

*No Journey carries one far
unless it goes an equal distance
into the world within.*

— Lillian Smith

I was born attentive and concerned about money.

One of my earliest money memories is stealing from my best friend. I am ashamed to remember that at age eight, I was a thief.

It was a moment of private show and tell. The kind kids engage in when they want to one-up each other. I was mesmerized as she smugly dumped out the contents of her piggy bank. There it was, a heap of shimmering silver, copper and nickel. The coins twinkled in my eyes. As they say in the South, I felt like I had died and gone to heaven. I wanted to have money too. She had so much, surely no one would notice if I took a little of her change.

> "*I wanted to* have *money, too.*"

Interestingly, once I stole the money, I saved it. Buying things was not my style. I just wanted to *have* money. So once I had taken my best friend's allowance, I put it in my underwear drawer. Surely a safe and stable resting place for my first and last heist, or so I thought.

But my mother discovered my newly acquired assets. She confronted me in a gentle and kind way. After our talk, she came to see how important having my own money was, and my allowance was born.

Soon after my thievery, I too acquired a piggy bank. Whenever money came my way, I saved it. My allowance, birthday money, the two dollars I earned from raking leaves, the quarter my grandfather gave me on his occasional visit, the penny I found on the street; all ended up in my piggy bank.

One of my favorite pastimes was counting the change in my bank. I always engaged in this ritual alone in my room. I would lie on my bed and turn my bank upside down. Using a kitchen knife, I would cajole the pennies, nickels, dimes and my prized possessions, quarters, out of the jar and onto my stomach. I loved the feel of money falling onto my belly.

After the jar was empty, I sorted the money into like kind, pennies in one pile, nickels in another and so forth. Then I would make stacks of each kind of coin into dollar equivalents. Finally I would count the dollars and loose change carefully, several times.

When my piggy bank was full, I would take the contents down to the local savings and loan and deposit it into my passbook account. Unlike my friends, I never spent money on soda, junk food, or stuff. I was a serious saver.

At age fourteen, I began working. I was driven to have my own money. I was clear that I did not want to be a financial burden to anyone.

Where did this burning desire to be financially independent come from? It seemed that it was just always there. With it, I fit right into our get-it-done, workaholic culture. I was ambitious and hard-working.

My passion to be self-reliant served me well. I accomplished my childhood goal and earned the majority of my own money for college. As soon as I graduated, I began a regular savings program. By the age of thirty-five, I had a successful business that I had started on a shoestring. I was living a life of financial prosperity beyond what I had dreamed of in my youth.

> " *I loved the feel of money falling onto my belly.* "

These were the symptoms of my money life:

- My business was receiving awards for top-line growth.

- I saved regularly.

- I invested my savings wisely.

- I had no credit card debt.

- I was living in a house well below my means.

- I was generous in meeting others' needs.

And

- My business profits were substantially less than my peers.

- I rarely spent money on myself, and when I did it was "on sale."

- I often negotiated contracts where I was on the short end of receiving.

I was living a life of financial prosperity beyond what I had dreamed of in my youth.

What was missing was an ability to stand for myself. Even the motivation for what looked like taking care of myself — my savings plan — was to assure I was not a burden.

As a result of an inward journey to discover myself, I found the source of my intense sense of responsibility. I found it using a tool called the Enneagram and by exploring the events of my past.

At the age of five my mother explained to me that I was adopted. She said my birth parents were young and didn't have enough money for a baby. She said they loved me very much, and that they demonstrated that love by giving me away to new parents.

To me the message was clear. If you cost too much, people will abandon you. Ask for very little and take care of yourself.

I am not saying this is what my parents told me. I am saying that this is what I interpreted from my conversation with my mother. My child's perspective was to become my adult reality.

Prosperity Insight

The Enneagram is a powerful and dynamic personality system that describes nine distinct and fundamentally different patterns of thinking, feeling, and acting. It tells us what motivates us, what basic coping strategies we adopt to survive and thrive, and what causes our relationships to flourish or flounder. In addition, the Enneagram provides a specific path of personal development and enrichment for each of the nine types — ways to discover our highest qualities and purpose in life. **http://www.authenticenneagram.com**.

This belief became a habit and permeated everything in my life. My savings and investment accounts, living below my means, my conservative lifestyle, all were results driven by my world view. Depending on someone else terrified me.

I was on automatic due to my own programming. To be fully present to joy in my life, I had to first recognize that I was acting out of habit, and then shift to choosing deliberately. I had to move into creating my life through choice in the present moment rather than responding to life out of my learned patterns.

The Enneagram became the system I used to name, label and then begin to unwind my automatic programming. I read, studied and took classes. I became a certified Enneagram teacher in the oral tradition. As part of this study, I began a regular meditation program. Soon my ability to self-observe became comfortable and easily accessible. Now rather than being locked into a habitual pattern, I used my new skills to choose for me.

So here I am at forty-seven. I am clear that asking for very little has served me well in the past. My journey is to release the fear of receiving, and to claim my own worthiness in the process. Now I make conscious choices in the present moment. As I do, everything in my life shifts, and I have access to true joy.

Yet letting go of a past that is known, even if it is not working, is scary stuff. It requires a leap of faith. This book is a path for all those who want to take a leap of faith and make their own journey to *The Intersection of Joy and Money*.

My personal belief is that we are all here to make a difference in our time on this earth. I believe I was called to show people how to shift their money conversations. As you unwind your patterns about money, you will shift many other aspects of your life.

Take a leap of faith. Let go of your past and enjoy the journey. What waits for you is JOY, the kind that comes from deep within yourself. ∎

2

Intersection: A place where two lines cross

Joy: A very glad feeling; delight

Money: Property, possessions, or wealth

*The future belongs to those
who believe in the beauty
of their dreams.*

— Eleanor Roosevelt

*T*he Intersection of Joy and Money happens when you are present to both joy and money simultaneously in the now. This is true prosperity.

Prosperity moments can be elusive. Rather than joy, you experience fear. You may

- Worry about having enough

- Be concerned about running out

- Wonder if you are deserving

Or

- Freeze into inaction when decisions are needed about money.

Fear, in and of itself, precludes joy.

Culturally you have been taught that the road to prosperity is about having an abundance of money. But is this true? Affluent people have fears too. They worry about making their money last, leaving enough to their kids, or how their pile or possessions compare to their friends. These are not prosperity conversations. These are different faces of fear.

Where do all these fears come from? Primarily from informal training by your family, all of whom had their own bias and dysfunction about money.

Ever watch very young children? They live in the moment. When they have a need they express it. If they hurt, they cry. If someone hurts them, they respond. Their reactions are genuine and spontaneous. In addition, after the upset is over they are complete. They don't hold onto displeasure.

You began in innocence. But as you grew up, you came to see that the world was conditional. You got approval for certain reactions and disapproval for others. Naturally you gravitated to approval. You developed behaviors to cope with and get approval within your environment. Soon, these behaviors were so entrenched they seemed like they were always present. You developed a habit of mind.

To experience prosperity you have to identify and bring into awareness your habits of mind. Most people, whether they are wealthy, middle class, or debt-ridden, lack consciousness about their conversations, beliefs, patterns and habits around money. The patterns by which you run your money life are so familiar that you cannot clearly articulate them.

> *You co-create your entire life, including your money life, through choice.*

To shift your prosperity thinking requires a journey of self-discovery. You must explore your past to identify your programming. You will find the source of your fears, and the habits of mind you developed to cope with them. Once you have done so, you can begin to unwind your habits and replace them with present-moment consciousness.

You co-create your entire life, including your money life, through choice. Yet until you begin to self-observe, you make these choices through an unrecognized filter or habit of mind. This is what is meant by unconsciousness. It is similar to wearing a pair of red glasses so you see the world in shades of red. But your neighbor has a green pair so she sees the world in tones of green. Until you expose your past conditioning, you are unaware of the shade of your view, and at the same time, you believe incorrectly that everyone else sees as you do.

Getting to *The Intersection of Joy and Money* is a journey to discover yourself and unlock your past. It is about moving from reacting to creating by continually growing and expanding in your awareness of yourself. Along the way you enhance your ability to make conscious choices.

You must travel five paths to complete this journey:

- Path One, Self-referencing and conscious choice
- Path Two, Responsibility and reality
- Path Three, Goals and strategies
- Path Four, Congruent action
- Path Five, Re-assessment

Path One
Self-referencing and conscious choice

Joy in your money life requires self-referencing. We live in a society where everywhere we turn — TV, radio, the Internet, billboards, the neighbors — there are messages about the road to happiness via product or service purchases.

Joy isn't in a car, or a house, or anywhere except inside you. In order to fit in or look good, if you have to send your kids to a particular school, drive a specific car, belong to the country club, or wear a certain brand of clothes, you are not in prosperity thinking.

On the contrary, if you are able to look for yourself and see what really takes care of you, then you are in prosperity thinking. Your spending and saving

> *The only path to prosperity is to take parts we consider classified out of the closet and discard them.*

should support and nurture you, not just on the surface level of *keeping up with the Joneses* but at a deeper level that says, *This fulfills my desires.* You are blocked from self-referencing by your current habits of mind. That is why deciding to choose for yourself isn't so simple. First you have to look at your history and bring into awareness the messages you took on as truth. Then you have to look at the behaviors you developed around your truth. Lastly you have to learn to choose again, this time for yourself in the present moment.

Path Two
Responsibility and reality

Joy requires self-responsibility. As a human being, one of the ideas you have seen modeled is to blame others for your circumstances. You learned to be a victim. When you play the *if only* game, you are attempting to shift the responsibility for the results in your life to someone else.

As the co-creator of your life, there is no one else to blame for your results. If you are generating debt you can never repay, this is your choice. If you whine about how undervalued you are in your job, while doing nothing to change your work environment, this is your choice. If you complain about how irresponsible your children are, yet continually bail them out, this is your choice.

We all have things we are ashamed of in our money life. To protect ourselves, we hide the embarrassing parts. Unfortunately, keeping secrets holds the old energy in place and keeps us from fully self-expressing. The only path to prosperity is to take parts we consider classified out of the closet and discard them.

People often play a game called *Let's pretend*. It is a convenient game of hiding out to assure yourself of not having the life you want. *Let's pretend* is a game of avoidance and can be used to allow you to be a victim of your environment in any situation. Adults often indulge in this game.

A typical game of *Let's pretend* occurs when people are unfulfilled in their jobs. They say, *I cannot afford to leave this job, I cannot live on less, I cannot sell my business, as I have to support myself,* and so on. Generally they have not taken the time to look at their financial situation to see if any of this is true. They invent the truth they need to keep themselves from risk and real change.

People who have joy around money are in total reality about their money. They are clear about how money comes in and how it goes out. If they have a choice to make, they look to see if they have the financial resources to support their choice. If not, they commit to shifting whatever it takes to make their dreams come true. They do not play the game of *Let's pretend*.

Path Three
Goals and strategies

At *The Intersection of Joy and Money* you are clear about your goals. Most of us have an easier time articulating what we don't want. There is something about claiming our wishes that is scary.

Wants are not just about effects and possessions. You get things because of what you think they will provide you, a certain feeling, convenience, fun. Those feelings or outcomes are your true goals.

The goal isn't a new car. The goal is what the new car gives you. At the simplest level, it gives you transportation. It may also give you prestige. And sometimes a new car makes you feel new again. You get that feeling of *I can do anything* that you experienced as a teenager. The true goal then is reliable transportation, prestige, or the feeling of being young again. The car is the strategy to get the goal.

The path to prosperity requires that you clearly identify and claim for yourself your goals. Once identified, you may find they presently exist in your life in many forms. In addition, you will discover a diversity of strategies to manifest your dreams.

> *Action is the vehicle to your new money life.*

Path Four
Congruent action

Of course none of this will work unless you take action. You may be great at conceiving a new idea, or researching the best stock to buy, but without action nothing really shifts. Staying in your head with your ideas is a way to avoid risk. Changing your life requires that you feel the fear and do it anyway. Action is the vehicle to your new money life.

How you make, spend and invest your money, is your money in action. It is an expression of you and your value system. When your actions are in alignment with your beliefs you are in integrity. With every action you have an opportunity to choose. Once you are clear about what serves you around money, you can choose with consciousness for yourself.

Path Five
Re-assessment

Lastly, to live your life at *The Intersection of Joy and Money*, you have to re-assess. You may be on the path and then get off track. That is life. You get off track in every aspect of your life from time to time.

You may let your health degenerate. You know you need to exercise regularly, but things come up. Time gets scarce. The next thing you know it has been six months, a year, and you haven't exercised. So what do you do? Well you could say, *Why start now?* But if you really want to get back in shape, the only thing to do is to begin exercising again.

When your money life gets off track, the only thing to do is to start again from wherever you are. Simply choose again. ■

Summary

You are at *The Intersection of Joy and Money* when:

✔ You are responsible.

✔ You are self-referenced.

✔ You are clear about your goals.

✔ You have strategies for accomplishing your goals.

✔ You are making conscious choices.

✔ You are in congruent action.

✔ You re-assess, check in, and review your outcomes.

✔ You are able to choose again.

3
Money
Fantasies

*There's a gigantic difference
between earning a great deal
of money and being rich.*

— Marlene Dietrich

We all have fantasies about money. What exactly are money fantasies and where did they come from? A money fantasy is a false belief or learned money conversation. You were taught these beliefs formally or informally. Though they are learned rules you took them on as truth.

The level of prosperity you have achieved is a creation of these false beliefs. Not reaching your full potential, being constantly over-committed in debt, not being able to fully enjoy your wealth — these come from learned money conversations. You use these false beliefs to form the basis of your choices and decisions, and as a result, your life.

You generated these fantasies by watching, listening and experiencing others in your environment. Your parents, grandparents, teachers, and peers gave you advice and counsel based on their own experience. They passed on to you the rules they knew about money. But who taught them the rules? Did they work? Did their rules get them to *The Intersection of Joy and Money*?

We also have fantasies generated from the media, whose agenda includes your acting in a way in which they profit. It doesn't mean they are bad, just that they are acting from their own self-interest. Your job is to discern what is right for you.

Prosperity is an inside job. So often you take what you hear or see and make it truth, without really stopping to see if it works for you. To discover your truth, consider the information, capture the parts that are relevant and discard the rest. Taking information directly from any source without running it through your own filter keeps you from prosperity. Only you know what joy is for you.

Here are some common fantasies:

Time is money.

You have heard and perhaps even said, *Time is money.* Have you ever stopped to examine this? The truth is, time is not money. By holding onto this fantasy you create an unnecessary boundary around your prosperity.

This is a self-limiting belief that to receive more money, you must put in more time. It is a convenient fantasy to keep you on the treadmill called *work*.

What is true is that money represents the value of what is provided, whether you are looking at your paycheck, or a new necklace. The amount of money exchanged in any interaction is equal to the value each person perceives in the exchange.

Consider this simple example. You are hiring a CPA to do your taxes. One tells you his or her fee is $100 per hour, the second $250 per hour and requires that you do annual tax planning in order to buy his or her services. The first CPA does not give you a fixed price. The second gives you a fixed price of $1000 a year and the option to pay quarterly.

Who do you hire? What is it that you want? If you simply want your return prepared, perhaps the first CPA is the best choice. But how many hours will he spend? Do you want to buy services when you really don't know the total cost?

Do you want someone to help you reduce your income taxes in a proactive way? If so, the second CPA might be the best choice. And what if that CPA's planning saved you $1000 a year, or $2000, or even as little as $500? You may very well end up with more cash in your pocket as a result of investing in quality advice.

The truth is that what someone charges per hour is not really relevant. What is important is what you need and want, and the value you place on getting those needs and wants met. With this perspective, you can choose what really works for you.

Debt is bad.

The truth is debt is bad when it is a substitute for living within your means. Using credit for everyday household items such as clothing and groceries is just a way of spending more than you make. Plastic is easy money. It doesn't appear real. Unfortunately, using a card is simple. Repaying it is not. Never charge more than you can pay off each month; otherwise, you are creating a trap for yourself, one that can easily end in bankruptcy.

Prosperity Insight

If using credit cards to overspend is a habit of yours, convert to cash instead. Take your credit cards out of your purse or wallet. For every paycheck withdraw from your account what you can afford to spend, that is, what you don't need for your regular bills. Then, when you spend, do so with cash. You will notice an immediate shift in how you relate to spending. It will take on a reality that was missing when you used plastic.

When you borrow to acquire an asset that generates a return, this is good debt. Return may take the form of rents, profits, interest, dividends, appreciation or royalties. For example, if you buy a building to expand your business, you need debt. By expanding your business, your profits from the business will increase. In this case, you have used debt as a vehicle to ultimately increase your cash flow.

You may also invest in yourself, by furthering your knowledge or skills. This in turn provides you the opportunity to increase the value of your contribution in the world, and, as a result, your return. Debt to increase your own personal contribution may be good debt, as long as your increased earnings are sufficient to repay the debt you incurred.

I will save after I pay off my debt.

Many of us begin our adult life with debt. You may have student loans. You may have credit card debt that you accumulated before you realized just how hard it is to pay off.

The way your debt arose isn't important. The question is, How do you repay it? Should you repay it as quickly as you can, and then save? Or should you begin saving now? The answer generally is to begin saving now. It really depends on your age, how much more time you have to save, and whether the interest you pay is deductible. To truly find the best answer for you, you have to do a little math.

The choices are to pay the debt or to save. Do not confuse this with paying debt or spending. If you do

Prosperity Insight

Money compounds by the Rule of Seventy-two. That is, seventy-two divided by your rate of return tells you how fast your money will double. Using twelve percent as an example, your money will double every six years (72÷12=6). That means if you have $10,000 you will have $20,000 in six years. If you have $100,000 you will have $200,000 in six years.

Obviously $200,000 is more exciting than $20,000. How do you accumulate $100,000 in order to double? By getting started. By saving now. You have to get started from wherever you are. Once you do, your money will double. Of course if you never start, it never will.

not have the discipline to save money, focus on paying your debt. In all cases, if you are not saving at all, start saving something. If you choose the course of paying debt as quickly as possible, still save something, as little as $10 a week. Saving money is investing in your future. Paying off old debt is healing your past. Both are required.

To determine the best path requires an analysis of the cash flow necessary with each alternative you are considering.

Discern your answer by running the numbers. You cannot assume that you know which path produces the best result.

My home is an investment.

This means when you retire, you plan to sell your house, move into a rental unit, and use the proceeds to support yourself. It could also mean you plan to sell your residence and buy a much less expensive one at retirement. Unless one of these alternatives is true for you, your home is not an investment; it is a lifestyle choice.

Often this is a convenient fantasy used to justify the purchase of a home that costs more than you can afford. It

Prosperity Insight

Assume you have $5,000 in credit card debt. You have $500 a month in cash flow from your paycheck to either service the credit card or fund your 401(k). The minimum credit card payment is $100. Your interest rate on your credit card is 18%. You earn 10% on your investments. Your income tax rate is 30%. Which alternative is best, pay the credit card off as soon as possible, or pay the credit card off more slowly, while funding your 401(k)?

The first question is do you have $500 a month for both alternatives? It would seem so. And if there were no such thing as income taxes, this would be the correct answer.

However, because Congress wants to encourage retirement savings, you get a tax deduction for 401(k) contributions. Therefore the alternatives are not as simple as they seem.

Here is how it works. When you contribute to your 401(k), that outflow is tax-deductible, so if you pay $1.00 into the plan, it requires $1.00 in cash flow. When you pay credit card interest and principal, it is not tax-deductible. This means if you pay $1.00 on your credit card, you must generate $1.00 plus the taxes on $1.00 to make this payment.

Said another way, you generally get money by earning income. When you earn income, you pay income tax. So if you earn $1.50, and our income tax is 30%, you pay 45 cents ($1.50X30%) in income tax, leaving you with a net cash flow of $1.05. So every time you pay
continued...

Prosperity Insight (*continued*)...

more credit card debt, it takes more gross cash flow to service the debt. Conversely if you use your cash flow to fund your 401(k), it only takes $1.00, because this is a tax-deductible outflow.

To find the best alternative for any situation requires that you run the numbers. You must consider income tax effects for your analysis to be valid. In the credit card debt example above, if you pay your credit card debt slower, and use the extra cash flow to fund your 401(k), it takes almost eight years to completely pay off your credit card debt, and you have accumulated about $51,500. If you pay your credit card debt as quickly as possible, and then use the entire cash flow to save, you generate just over $55,300. (Both illustrations are earning 10%).

However, the results differ dramatically when longer time frames are involved. If you do the same analysis for a fifteen vs. a thirty-year mortgage, even though you pay half a percentage point higher rate of interest on the thirty-year loan, you accumulate significantly more if you take the longer loan and save the difference. The person who takes the fifteen-year mortgage and then saves the difference accumulates just over $1.2 million when income tax effects are included in the analysis. The person who takes the thirty-year mortgage and saves the difference in the payment, plus the income tax benefits, accumulates over $2.1 million, or 75% more for the same cash flow.

may also allow you to justify additions or upgrades to your home. Unfortunately, pretending that spending money on your home is an investment will not get you to *The Intersection of Joy and Money.*

This is not to say it is wrong to spend money on your home. Do so with the clarity that your decision is a way of life, not an investment decision.

I will never be able to save enough, so why start?

Saving requires foregoing an indulgence in the present to have an opportunity for an alternative future. When you start saving it may seem that you will never accumulate enough to make a difference. The feeling that you will never make it can keep you blind to the other truth: In order to stop working, you have to accumulate assets to replace your paycheck. It may be painful to look at your savings reality. Do it anyway. Go beyond the criticism you will inevitably feel and begin or increase your savings today.

Buying stock is risky, so I will buy real estate, annuities, life insurance, or certificates of deposit.

The truth is that no one investment philosophy gives you as much foundation as buying a variety of investments. What works best is having a diversified portfolio of many kinds of assets, which includes stocks. Your mother was right when she said, *Don't put all your eggs in one basket.*

I don't need to know about this; I will hire someone.

The truth is that you may need or want to hire someone to help you with certain aspects of your finances. You may want to hire someone to coordinate your money life with the rest of your life. Each of us has unique skills and talents, and your abilities may not be in the financial area. On the other hand, you may have considerable skills in the area of money, but your life is overflowing with responsibilities at work and home.

Prosperity Insight

The **American Association of Individual Investors** specializes in providing education in the area of stock investing, mutual funds, portfolio management and retirement planning. AAII is a not-for-profit organization that arms investors with the knowledge and tools needed to manage their finances effectively and profitably. If you are new to the world of investing, or are looking for a source to learn more, check them out at **http://www.aaii.com**. There are also local chapters of AAII. Review the web site to see if there is one in your area.

When you do hire someone, you need to understand his or her advice and be able to see how it corresponds to your goals and strategies. This is your life. You are accountable for it. Be sure you are delegating, not abdicating.

I don't have to be responsible today; I'll make a lot of money tomorrow.

Perhaps you will be one of those fortunate people for which this is true. For most of us however, our wants can easily exceed our cash flow regardless of our income level. So putting off saving becomes a never-ending game that ultimately presents real challenges and very difficult choices as you age. When you postpone savings, you are choosing to make it hard on yourself.

Prosperity Insight

If a twenty-year-old who saves $2000 a year from age twenty to forty, quits saving at age forty, at age sixty she will have accumulated over $900,000 if she is able to generate a 10% rate of return.

If a forty-year-old that has saved nothing until the age of forty, begins saving, and saves $4000 a year from age forty to sixty, she accumulates less than $300,000 if she is able to generate a 10% rate of return.

So the forty-year-old saves twice as much money, and has a third less at retirement. The moral to the story is if you postpone your savings plan, it is hard to catch up, even if you double your efforts!

What we know to be truth is that the earlier you begin saving, the less you have to save to accumulate your "pile." Remember the Rule of Seventy-two? If you think about this rule, a person at twenty has many more years for her money to double than the person at fifty, who has to save a lot more. The fantasy is thinking you don't make enough to save. The truth is you do. You just have to decide to pay yourself first.

Why not ask for an IRA contribution as a birthday or holiday present? Or commit to yourself to bag your lunch once a week, putting the savings in your 401(k). There are many creative ways to find the cash flow to save. Make it easy on yourself; use the power of compounding, save early and often.

I have so much credit card debt; it is hopeless.

You are answerable for your debt; it was generated out of your old money habits. It is true that your situation is hopeless if you do nothing to alter these habits. If you are tired of the effects of excess debt on your life, there are three steps necessary to break the pattern.

Step One: Look at what spending money provides you. What are you attempting to get from the things you are acquiring?

Step Two: Distinguish between your goals and strategies. You will do this in the exercises in Chapter Eight. This will provide you with clarity to focus on what is really important.

Step Three: Commit to do whatever it takes to pay off your debt and live within your means. That could mean taking on a second job, working overtime, turning a hobby into income, or making do with your old car instead of a new one.

The exercises in this book will walk you through Steps One and Two. Step Three requires you leave the victim mode and move into taking charge of your life.

Prosperity Insight

To pay off your credit card debt in the most efficient manner, start by making a list of your debts in four columns; card name, balance, interest rate and minimum payment. Take the credit card on which you owe the least, and put all your extra cash toward this debt. Pay the minimum on the other balances. When that card is paid in full, begin on the debt that was the second lowest balance. Take the amount you were paying on the card that you paid off, add the minimum payment on the new card, and pay that until this card is paid off. Continue this process until all your cards are paid off. Each time you pay a card off, do something you really love that costs you nothing — a walk in the woods, a trip to the library, extra time with your family. While engaged in this activity hold a blessing for yourself and the courage you demonstrated by making your life different.

My consciousness isn't required for my investments to grow.

My experience has been that when people have this money fantasy, they usually end up with a bunch of investments they do not understand, cannot explain, and which are not very well suited to their personal situation. The people who have been served are the sellers of the investments. They received commissions on the sale: once sold, they provided no follow-up or overview of the investment. This is certainly not always true, but more often than not.

If your investments don't work, you are the one who will suffer. Hiring an advisor is a responsible action, one that requires homework. You need to understand the advisor's philosophy and see that it is congruent with your own. You also have to understand how this advisor gets paid, and in what you are investing.

Buying stuff is an investment.

Beanie babies, Hummels, jewelry, artwork, guns: You name it and someone is out there justifying his or her purchase as an investment. Be straight with yourself. If you really want to indulge yourself, do so with that intention. Continuing to pretend holds your old patterns in place.

Look clearly at what your purchases really provide you. Then choose with consciousness.

Shopping is fun and I won't deprive myself.

The truth is that not depriving yourself has its own kind of deprivation, the type where you have to work forever. This fantasy takes away your choices. You will never be able to slow down, take an extended vacation, or start your own business because you cannot afford the dip in cash flow these choices produce. You are trapped on the treadmill of labor.

I am going to work till I die.

Good luck. Perhaps you know more than most of us about when your final moment is coming. The truth is you may not be physically capable of working until you die. Having no savings or investment plan keeps you in the confining pattern of work. Having a savings and investment plan gives you choices, options, and freedom.

I don't spend a lot of money, and I will spend less in retirement.

First, before you declare that you don't spend a lot of money now, look at what you do spend. Most people are surprised when they take the time to look at their cash flow in black and white. Whatever you need or want is okay. You do not need to judge it or allow anyone else to. The important point is to be clear about what you really require and take responsibility for creating it.

Look clearly at what your purchases really provide you. Then choose with consciousness.

Second, when you retire, you have more leisure time. How will you fill that time? With travel, hobbies, or volunteering? Some of these activities may cost you more than you are currently spending. Make your decision from a place of reality. Look at your current spending and ask yourself whether it would be less in retirement.

I will marry money.

Do you really want to bank your future on someone else? Stop and consider your own sense of self-worth. What would the feeling be to provide for yourself? What kind of relationship will you have if you can't afford to stand on your own two feet?

I am waiting for my family to leave me an inheritance.

The truth is, *The Intersection of Joy and Money* is a place of self-responsibility. Treat an inheritance as a possibility, not a certainty; then either way, you have taken care of yourself.

I will depend on social security.

Prosperity Insight

Find out more about social security at **http://www.ssa.gov**.

First, be very clear that collecting social security is dependent on future generations paying in enough payroll tax to support the retired population. Just looking at the truth of our country's demographics may change your mind about living on social security.

Second, do you really want to live at that level of income? Before you say yes, review your personal

Prosperity Fable

Dr. Skinner was 62 when we met. He was making $170,000 a year, his kids were grown and on their own, and he and his wife had moved into a smaller home near the country club. At first glance he appeared ready for retirement, or at least scaling back his practice. He told me his immediate needs were income tax planning and accounting assistance.

However, a few weeks into our work together, another need appeared: cash flow. His payable clerk called to say there was not enough money to pay the bills. As I inquired, I found this was a recurring pattern. The symptoms of Dr. Skinner's money life unfolded: forty years of excessive spending, followed by increasing debt. He would ultimately pay off his credit cards by refinancing his home.

As I gathered more information, the facts became even more alarming.

Dr. Skinner frequently did not fund his pension plan because of insufficient cash flow. As a result, at 62, he had $200,000 in his pension plan, not even enough assets to cover his retirement for two years. He was often behind with his creditors and overextended on his line of credit.

He took no responsibility for his spending habits. He insisted that he had no other options. I worked with him for three years, attempting to bring some reality into the picture. No matter what we tried, he insisted on being a victim of his circumstances, while at the same time, blaming everyone else for his situation. I finally decided to end our working relationship, as I knew that until he chose to change, his life would continue on this pattern of increasing debt. Years later at age 72, he is still on the treadmill called *work*.

social security statement, which gives you an estimate of the monthly benefit amounts you and your family may qualify for now and in the future. You receive this statement annually from the Social Security Administration.

I will win the lotto.

Good luck. You might also try standing outside with an umbrella in a thunderstorm. Actually your chances of getting hit by lightning are better than winning the lotto.

If I have lots of money I will be happy.

I am sure you have heard the old saying, *Money can't buy happiness*. It is as true today as ever. Money is necessary in our society to have our needs met. Yet joy is an inside job. You have to do the inside work first, and then you will have the tools to explore your options for happiness.

Sacrifice is necessary.

If you have taken this fantasy on as truth, life may look pretty hard and grim. Another possibility is that you are confusing goals and strategies. (Chapter Eight gives you the tools to clearly delineate these terms.) While it may be necessary for you to postpone acquiring a possession, that may not mean you can't have what the possession provides you through another avenue. Distinguishing goals and strategies gives you the power to choose from your highest desires.

Work is hard, boring, a chore. I can't wait to retire.

There are only three legal ways to get money. Marry it, inherit it or make it. You probably already know if you married it or are going to inherit. If these are not options for you then what is left is to make it.

When you make money you do so at work. Isn't it interesting that we call it *work*, a word synonymous with effort and labor? You were raised in a model that says success comes from hard work. Toil and labor until you are fifty-five, sixty or sixty-five. Scrimp, save and retire to somewhere sunny. Play golf, have cocktails at lunch and enjoy the good life.

There is another possibility. Work is not difficult. Work is pure joy. By finding the essence you have within and combining it with your passion, your work is effortless. It is easy. It is simple. It is pure joy.

Your essence represents the gift(s) with which you were born. You did not have to go to school or be trained to acquire your essence. Your passion is what energizes you about your legacy to the world. What do you feel passionate about contributing to humanity? In the days past, many people used the term *vocation* to describe the concept of combining something that nurtures your soul with the activity that brings you money. You do not have to be a minister, priest or rabbi to be fulfilled at work.

You need not dread going to work. You can rejoice in it. It is not necessary to count down the days to retirement. When your work is born of your passion and essence, why would you retire? Retirement is a time when your hopes and dreams come true. But why wait? Why not have them come true now, by creating a business or job that stems from your essence and passion?

> *By finding the essence you have within and combining it with your passion, your work is effortless.*

There are as many forms of false learning about money as there are people on this planet. Here are a few more fantasies you may find on your list:

- It is better to give than to receive.

- To have money is to be selfish.

- Rich people are not good people.

- Keep your dreams small, so as not to be disappointed.

- Girls should not be as successful as boys.

Whatever your fantasies, they are operating in your life whether you are aware of them or not. To shift your prosperity find out what false beliefs you took on, then choose to let them go. If this is what you desire, keep reading. And do all the exercises in the book! ■

Summary

- ✔ You have money fantasies.

- ✔ Your money fantasies were generated by watching, listening, and experiencing these in your environment.

- ✔ Holding onto money fantasies keeps you from prosperity.

- ✔ The first step in letting go of your fantasies is to identify them.

- ✔ Prosperity is an inside job.

Chapter

4

Money
Truths

*Everybody must learn this lesson
somewhere – that it costs something
to be what you are.*

— Shirley Abbott

What we believe to be true about money usually is not *truth*. A *truth* is true even if you doubt it, and it applies universally to every one of us, all the time.

What you believed in the past to be true about money is money fantasy. A money fantasy is true only because you accept it. It does not apply unanimously; rather it operates one way for some and differently for others.

The energy that you have used to hold your own personal money fantasies in place is available to you to transform your relationship with money to one of prosperity. As you begin to identify and unwind your fantasies, you allow money truths to come into your life.

There are five basic money *truths*.

Truth One
You are responsible for your money life.

The first money truth is that you are responsible for your money life, just as you are responsible for all your life. When you fail to take responsibility you are playing the role of a victim, and there is no such thing as a joyous victim.

The word *responsibility* may bring up negative images such as burden, heavy, duty, obligation, or sacrifice. There are alternative expressions of responsibility. One expression is to respect and honor yourself, recognizing your own worth and value in the world. You have much to contribute, and when you find the right match for your gifts, you will be rewarded.

> *The energy that you have used to hold your own personal money fantasies in place is available to you to transform your relationship with money to one of prosperity.*

> *Attention alters reality. You may choose to attend to limitation or you may choose instead to appreciate your abundance.*

Allowing yourself to be less than your possibility is a form of irresponsibility. Being proud of yourself, being clear about your talents, and valuing them is honoring the self. You cannot truly pay tribute to others until you have honored yourself. This is not selfish; this is self-responsible.

Responsibility is also about being in the flow. When you recognize that giving and receiving are different facets of the same thing and begin to celebrate the joy in both, you are being responsible in your money life.

Another feature of money accountability is the practice of gratitude. Like attracts like. Attention is a magnet. What you attend to manifests in your life. If you are negative and focus only on what you do not have, you are attending to lack and will bring more scarcity into your life. On the contrary if you appreciate what you do have, withholding your own mind's judgment about its limitations, you will attract abundance into your life.

Attention alters reality. You may choose to attend to limitation or you may choose instead to appreciate your abundance. Whatever your choice, you will create your money life from it.

If you have given away responsibility for your money life, look again. Joy comes to those who accept and celebrate self-responsibility.

Truth Two
Your consciousness is required for money health.

Lack of consciousness is expressed on two levels.

The first is found whenever you pretend something about your money life without looking to see if it is true. You make up things about money as a way of keeping your present reality in place.

You may keep secrets in your money life, or you may avoid looking at your financial facts. Both behaviors are driven by fear. You pretend that if you avoid reality the fear will go away, but it keeps an ever-vigilant guard. Dodging the fear looks like safety, but it really serves to keeps you stuck in your present reality. Only by feeling the fear and doing the very thing you are afraid of, will the fear dissipate.

Here are some examples of avoiding reality, being stuck in fear, and staying unconscious in your money life:

- Never finding the time to look at how you receive and spend money.

- Hiring an advisor without doing your homework.

- Failing to ask your advisor how she or he gets paid, for fear of embarrassing yourself or your advisor.

- Not having a clear relationship with your advisor by failing to put your expectations in writing, clearly articulating what takes care of you in your relationship.

- Pretending you understand your advisor's recommendations when you really cannot follow the conversation.

- Allowing an advisor to give advice when you have not spent any time discussing your goals and strategies.

- Never preparing an annual personal financial statement that outlines your assets and liabilities, clearly delineating your net worth.

- Never finding the time to do the exercises in this book or another tool, to discover your money fantasies.

- Overusing credit cards, pretending that you will pay the balance.

- Investing in companies that pollute the environment, when you are an adamant advocate of sustainable ecology.

- Not saving for a rainy day.

- Staying in a job you dislike because it pays really well.

- Not letting your talents shine.

- Holding on to a job you find unfulfilling because you have a family to support, because you have a mortgage, because you do not have a degree, because _____.

- Taking responsibility for your adult children's financial health and lifestyle.

- Not learning about money, the Rule of Seventy-two, the basics of investing, or how to manage a checkbook responsibly.

- Not teaching your children about money, the Rule of Seventy-two, the basics of investing, or how to manage a checkbook responsibly.

- Not saving for your own financial independence.

- Pretending that you do not make enough money to save, to fund your 401(k), your IRA, or your retirement plan.

Avoiding reality keeps you stuck in your present creation and leaves you feeling small, unseen, and unfulfilled. In the beginning accepting the challenge to walk through these fears may look like you are accepting a journey of unending panic. With courage and patience, as you walk through your fear, what you will find is yourself. You will say yes to life, filled with joy.

There is yet another subtler form of unconsciousness. Unless you have taken on the study of the Enneagram or a similar tool, you have a habit of mind of which you are unaware. This habit of mind, also called your personality or type, operates every minute of every day. Every interaction you have is filtered through this habit of mind. Every time you speak, act or respond, you have filtered your voice through your habit of mind.

Because these habits of mind are so familiar to you, it takes courage and introspection to discover and bring then into view. With practice you can begin to

" In the beginning accepting the challenge to walk through these fears may look like you are accepting a journey of unending panic. "

Prosperity Fable

Mary had a financially successful business that she ran four days a week. She used the other day to work on a business that she really loved. Unfortunately her new business was just getting off the ground and was losing, not making money. In our coaching sessions together Mary would say, *I can't wait to sell this business, but I can't right now, it pays the bills*. My response was, *Is this really true? You have savings, and if you sell your business you will have the proceeds to pay your bills*.

Yes, said Mary, *but I do not want to spend that money. I want to hold onto it.* To which I replied, *What if spending that money got you to the place you really want to be, working full time in your new business, and making more money in it than you do now?* Every session was closed with, *At our next appointment, let's really look at your money situation and see how you can afford to do what you want.*

Over several months this conversation continued, with Mary avoiding looking at whether she could live off her savings and the sale of her business, how long, and if that was truly an avenue to creating her new life. As a result, nothing in her life really changed. She was able to hold onto her story that she couldn't afford to sell her business. As a result she stayed stuck in her fear, creating the same reality day in and day out. She was working in a business she really didn't love in order to pay the bills, without enough time to get her new business up and running. Her payoff was that it was safe.

To do what was safe kept her from the possibility of reaching her dream. What if she failed? She might feel humiliated. What if she was financially successful beyond her wildest dreams? Her close relationships might change dramatically. But Mary didn't articulate these fears. They were hidden conveniently behind her story that she didn't have enough money.

You see, not having the money was just a very socially accepted way of not reaching for her dreams. Mary used her money fantasy to keep herself in a familiar place, but not where she really wanted to be. In so doing she avoided all the possible permutations of taking on her new identity. If Mary had been willing to look at her money reality, she would have seen that she could pay her bills for a year, before she ran out of money. Having observed the truth, she could decide if twelve months was enough to make her new business profitable. Then she could have put a business plan together to support her in her transition.

observe your personality rather than being trapped in it. Once you begin this practice of self-observation, you will be able to recognize your automatic response. Able to choose without the blinders of your personality, your choice takes on real power.

Truth generates an opening for creating the money life you want. The sooner you give up pretending and begin telling the truth about your relationship to money, the sooner you will manifest your dreams.

Prosperity Insight

Another avenue to accessing your own true nature is discussed in the book, *The Power of Now*, by Eckhart Tolle. This book does not use the Enneagram, but with Mr. Tolle's own words he describes how our minds keep us from who we really are, and from enjoying life as it was intended. You can read excerpts from his book at **http://www.eckharttolle.com**.

Truth Three
Each piece of your money life gives you the whole.

There are many facets to your money life. The teaching of Truth Three is that you must be responsible and conscious in each. The components of your money life are:

Money habits of mind

- What are your unrecognized patterns about money?

Goals and strategies

- What do you and your partner really want?

Current cash flow

- What is the source of your cash flow, and how are you spending it?

Future cash flow

- What are your needs in the future? How do you plan for them?

Planning for big-ticket items

- What's coming up, a new roof, a trip to Europe?

Current net worth

- What are your assets and liabilities?

Liquidity

- How much cash do you have? Can you keep yourself cash positive in an emergency, or in an economic downturn?

Risk management

- Have you protected yourself from unnecessary risk? Is your insurance adequate? Are you overpaying for insurance?

Financial independence

- What is your savings plan for retirement, or for financial independence?

Estate planning

- What if you passed away? Is your estate in order?

Income tax planning

- Do you pay the least amount of tax, legally?

College funding

- What do you want to provide for your children, grandchildren? What is your plan to do so?

Investment planning and management

- Are your investments managed in a way that supports your goals and strategies?

Aligning work with your essence and passion

- Do you get up each morning with the eager anticipation of doing what you love?

Paying attention to all aspects of your money life is needed. Focusing on just one area, no matter what it is, will not get you to *The Intersection of Joy and Money*. You have to consider each piece.

Prosperity Fable

John was significantly over-insured. At the age of sixty-five he had very little accumulated retirement savings and several large life insurance policies. It seemed one of his best golfing buddies, Sam, was a life insurance salesman. Every three to five years Sam would approach John, telling him about a great new policy. John would end up increasing his coverage, and Sam would collect large commissions. On the positive side, if John died, his family would be well taken care of. However, he had no personal options except to continue working. Sam was very motivated by his personal reward system. Unfortunately because they were friends, John did not get a second fee-based opinion, and so for years he over-paid for insurance, and under-funded his pension. As a result, John had no options except to continue working well past normal retirement age.

> *In your journey to your new money life, free yourself to discard any terms or ways of being that do not assist you.*

For example, it isn't enough to be well versed in investments and to disregard your need for insurance. Failing to insure appropriately can easily erase all your future plans. Without adequate disability insurance, you are putting yourself and your family at great risk. Conversely, it is not uncommon for people to overspend on life insurance. It is often sold out of fear, and generally with little education for the buyer. The result is less money for other areas of importance in your life.

What follows from Truth Three is that you can't possibly address all the facets of your financial life at the same time. First, identify your money fantasies. Next, clarify your goals and strategies. Subsequently, keeping your outcomes in focus, address each area, until you have looked at all aspects of your money life.

Truth Four
Choice is the ultimate power.

As humans we hold the ultimate power, choice. It is the power of creation. By accepting this power, you are acknowledging your creative gift. This is a universal truth. It operates in all of your life, including your money life.

As a culture, we do not actively teach the principle that your life is created through choice. We have even gone so far as to make choice seem like a burden. Look at the word *budget*. The very term brings up associations such as restriction, confinement, doing without, or lacking spontaneity. No one likes being on a budget. It is not seen as a joy-filled word.

But what is the true intention of a budget? At its core, it is simply a tool to help you choose how you want to spend your money. A budget helps you exercise the power of choice. Instead of budgets, make a Creation Plan, or use a term you find empowering. Throw away the word and use the essence of its purpose.

Another example where our historical teachings obscure choice is with a savings plan. For many people, saving seems like an obligation, and not a joyful one. It suggests doing without or sacrificing. But you can choose to save, and open yourself to the options that arise when you have a bankroll. Alternately, you can choose to stay on the work treadmill. There are only three ways legally to get money: marry it, inherit it, or make it. As we noted before, you already know if you have married it, or are going to inherit it, and if not, then you have to make it. You may choose to obligate yourself to work, or you may choose to free yourself by making the simple and powerful choice to save.

In your journey to your new money life, free yourself to discard any terms or ways of being that do not assist you. This is the process of discernment, choosing for your life those things that have value and leaving the rest. Notice that discernment is not judgment. It is simply choosing for yourself, implying no right or wrong, and distinguishing that which serves you.

Prosperity Insight

We know what we are, but know not what we may be. — **Shakespeare**.

When we take the power of creation and create avenues of restriction rather than use it to manifest abundance, we keep ourselves small and avoid our power.

Perhaps you feel locked into your choices by your circumstances: a spouse that does not work, a young child who needs your care, an elderly parent who requires your help. A good place to begin is to look at how you arrived at this place of no choice.

If you accepted responsibility to care for a partner, and now you find yourself resentful, perhaps you need to look again. Does it serve your partnership and your partner? It is rare to find a partnership where dissatisfaction of one partner is not matched by an equal frustration of the other. What will serve you in this circumstance is to accept responsibility for your feelings (without blame), gain clarity about your needs, and begin to articulate both your feelings and needs with love to your partner. Give them the same gift. Be present while they express themselves. Find the areas you have in common and look for creative ways for both parties to get what they want.

Another area where people feel they lack choice is in raising children. While you may feel strapped with the financial responsibility of their care, there are countless choices to be considered.

For example, it may or may not be necessary for your child to go to a private school. Or it may serve your child's future better when you are choosing not to purchase the hottest brand name clothes, and instead are investing the difference for her college education.

All of life is choice. And inside those choices if you fail to take care of yourself, you fail. The word *selfish* isn't a bad word. For only when you are totally taking care of yourself, in a powerful way, can you be present and giving to another. Anything less is self-delusion. Anything less, and you are giving your energy to the role of the victim.

This does not mean you are insensitive to the needs of others. It will often serve you to be generous. Just look to see if you are doing so from a place of true giving, expecting nothing in return.

Choose powerfully. If you are unhappy with your money life, simply choose again. This may not be easy, but it is simple.

> *The word* selfish *isn't a bad word.*

Truth Five
Money is energy and has value because we all agree that it does.

Money is a symbol of energy, power or life force. If you do not believe this, think about how much time you spend concerned about your money. How much effort you put into acquiring money. How many hours you consume spending money.

Consider your beliefs regarding money and power. Have you ever felt more in command of your life because you had a lot of money? Have you ever felt out of control when you lacked money? Have you ever been intimidated by someone you thought had significant wealth? Have you ever made yourself feel small or unimportant based on your paycheck?

You think of money as something tangible and real because you can hold it in your hands. But what are you really holding? A piece of paper printed by the government, or a brokerage statement that pronounces the value of your securities, or a bank statement reflecting how much cash you own.

All these pieces of paper reflect the value of something you own in dollars. But what is a dollar worth? A dollar is worth whatever the collective *we* agree upon. When you exchange money for something, it is because you feel that something is worth the dollars you are exchanging. You and the seller agreed and you do so every time you exchange money. What you are really agreeing on is how much of your energy you will exchange. The paper really has no value on its own.

You get attached to the value of your wealth expressed in dollars. Yet you have virtually no control over it. Is it any wonder that at many levels you feel out of control of your money life?

Here is a simple example. If you own land, it is worth what someone will pay for it. Until a buyer comes along, you can believe whatever you want about the value of the land. But someone must agree with you, and be willing to exchange money with you, for your land to have the value you perceive.

The same is true if you own stocks or securities. They have value because someone is willing to pay for them. You may look in the paper each night, or price your stocks on the Internet each day, to see what they are worth. But their value today is a result of what the collective buyers and sellers of that day

> *Money is a symbol of energy, power or life force.*

agreed upon. Tomorrow the agreement may be that your stocks are worth more or less.

Getting attached to the day-to-day value of your investments is a sure way not to be at *The Intersection of Joy and Money*. For each day *we*, that is, the buyers and sellers of that day, all agree your securities are worth more, you are happy. Each day *we* agree they are worth less, you are disappointed. You are keeping score in someone else's game and setting yourself up for unnecessary frustration and disappointment.

I am not saying that investing makes no sense. I am saying that investing is a long-term strategy, where you research and investigate your purchases, choosing them in congruence with your goals and strategies. Investing is a process where you purchase assets that send you a check, such as interest, dividends, or rents, and that may also have more value in the future than today. Do not deceive yourself. When you invest, realize that money has value because we all agree.

Looking at this truth clarifies why the concept of diversification is so important in your investment plan. Why? Because what the collective *we* wants changes. Sometimes we highly value large-cap growth stocks. Sometimes we highly value commodities such as gold. Events such as inflation, war, interest rates, etc, alter people's perspectives about the value of investments. Smart investing includes assets outside yourself, such as stocks, bonds, real estate, and commodities, and investments in yourself and your skills.

As you bring reality to your relationship with money, realize that money has a value we all agree upon. It is unlikely that you can control the common *we* agreement; therefore diversify. That includes investing in you. ∎

Summary

Let's review the Five Truths about money:

- ✔ You are responsible for your money life.

- ✔ Consciousness is required for money health.

- ✔ Being present to each piece of your money life gives you the whole.

- ✔ Choice is the ultimate power.

- ✔ Money is energy and has value because we all agree that it does.

When you manage your money life from the perspective of these *Five Truths*, you will be fully present to JOY.

5 Call to
Transformation

*A faith, confidence and
determination inside your
heart will not fail you.*

— Mary McLeod Bethune

By reading this book and doing the exercises, you will change your relationship to money. Unless you want to become conscious, responsible and accountable, do not pursue this material. Once you commit to change, everything in your life that does not work about money will arise. Your old patterns will try to make their last claim on you. Stay committed to your transformation and continue to work through the exercises.

Transformation occurs in layers. Even if you think you know yourself really well, going through these processes will peel off more layers, things you are holding onto that do not work.

Changing your relationship to money is a big step. Many people never get conscious around money. Fear gets in their way and keeps them stuck. Getting conscious is hard work, but it is the only path to having the money life you really want.

You have chosen to take a leap of faith. Faith in your ability to create your own future. Faith that you can look at what you don't want to see and choose again. Faith that you know how to take care of yourself. Faith that you are enough.

For money isn't just money. It may represent how you keep score, how you measure your self-esteem, or how secure you feel. Whatever money represents to you was learned out of your past conditioning. By reading this book and doing the homework, you are choosing to create your own scorecard, to find your inner voice, to create from within yourself.

> *You have chosen to take a leap of faith. Faith in your ability to create your own future.*

Looking deeply into the past will illuminate for you how you have built your patterns, beliefs, conversations and habits around money. You will see clearly how your past is creating your present. You will be amazed at your own interpretation of events from your past. The purpose of this work is not to point out your mistakes. The concept of right and wrong is self-defeating. The purpose is to bring your patterns into your consciousness so that you may observe them, determine if they are creating the money life you want, and if not, to choose again. By bringing this consciousness in and choosing your future, you create a new money foundation.

Along the way remember to be patient with yourself. Transformation, or lasting change, occurs in four steps:

Prosperity Insight

As you do this work, keep a journal of what you find and your feelings along the way. Journaling is a powerful tool that can create healing in many areas of your life, and money is no exception. The journal will also serve as a way to mark your progress. Part of being human is the need to recognize and celebrate your accomplishments. Writing regularly in a journal helps you remember where you started. Noticing your own progress is a great way to celebrate.

Step One
Unconscious incompetence

You are incompetent and are totally unaware that your life is not working. Circumstances outside you control your life. Someone else is at fault. *If only* is the cure to every ill. You feel unable to find the path to change.

Some ways to begin to transcend this step are:

- Set your intention.

- Get clear that you want a new relationship around money.

- Look clearly without judgment at your past.

- Be willing to dig deep.

Step Two
Conscious incompetence

You are incompetent, but you are aware that you are incompetent. This is a big step, a critical step, a step where you may choose to beat yourself up. Resist this urge. Instead celebrate your growth in becoming conscious. The stage of conscious incompetence is a difficult but necessary one. You cannot make lasting change without first recognizing your need to change.

A few helpful hints at this stage:

- Notice how the teachings of your past have created your habits, patterns, conversations and beliefs around money. See how your old teachings have you on autopilot. Notice how your old teachings limit you.

- Take on practices that support you in letting go of your old beliefs. Study the Enneagram. Meditate. Build a community. Share with your partner what you discover about yourself.

- The same patterns that are your habits of mind, are held in your physical body as well. Release old patterns in your body by engaging in some form of body work such as cranio-sacral therapy, Reiki, raindrop therapy, massage, or martial arts.

Step Three
Conscious competence

This is a challenging step. It requires moment-to-moment effort. You are now making new choices, but it requires an extraordinary amount of attention. It also requires forgiveness of self, as you will often relapse into your unconscious behavior. You are like a baby learning to walk. Celebrate every tiny step. Ignore your falls, realizing they are just part of your courage to grow.

The stage of conscious competence may look like this:

- Now that you can separate yourself from your beliefs, choose new beliefs in the present moment.

- Take a step of faith into the future. Do this by completing the exercises in this book. Do them thoroughly and with the intent to create a new prosperous reality. Even if an exercise doesn't make sense to you, do it anyway. This is the faith part. Don't skip steps and don't do them half-way. Put all your energy into each exercise, and be brutally honest with yourself in the process.

- Notice that what happens is called *chaos*. When you don't recognize something you name it *chaos*, but it is actually change. Be patient with the chaos, as it is your path. Don't waver, just keep moving forward. Embrace, celebrate and welcome the chaos. It is part of your creation process. Watch the transformation taking place. Journal.

When you don't recognize something you name it chaos, *but it is actually change*.

Prosperity Fable

Janet had a small service business. While she made enough income to manage, it was always a struggle. She was conscious enough to know that she did not know how to transform her relationship to money, and that she needed a coach to hold her accountable.

She was ready and committed to unwind her poverty conversations. Janet agreed to take my coaching and implement her new business plan. At first her business increased, cash flow improved, and everything looked rosy. Then I insisted she implement a fee increase.

She did so reluctantly and with fear that her clients would do business elsewhere. Her fears manifested, and business dropped off. But Janet stuck to her commitment to herself and to me as her coach, and continued to work her marketing plan. While her faith was sometimes shaky, she kept moving forward. Soon her business resumed and began to grow exponentially. Within three years Janet more than tripled her business. She stayed in action through all the stages of change, and in time, her self-esteem grew to meet her fee increase.

Step Four
Unconscious competence

Congratulations. Your change process is now complete. You now make new choices that support and nurture you. You are no longer reacting from your past; you are creating your future, moment to moment. From this place you can begin to grow to a new level, beginning at Step One again!

Some helpful ideas for this stage:

- Notice your new reality come into being. Notice when you feel empowered about money. Notice how more and more you are creating rather than reacting to your life around money.

■ Celebrate all your accomplishments, big and
small. Tell your friends; ask for their support.
Get and give hugs. Be lavish in appreciating
yourself. ■

Summary

The signals that tell you when you are living your life at *The Intersection of Joy and Money:*

✔ You are conscious. You make conscious choices.

✔ You are responsible. You take responsibility for your money life. Your actions around money are congruent with your personal values.

✔ You are clear about your goals. You have spent time developing them with your life partner. You know what you want.

✔ You have strategies to accomplish each goal, and they are prioritized.

✔ You are acting in congruence with your goals and strategies.

✔ You re-assess and periodically check in. You are open to new strategies. You take inventory to see if your actions are aligned with your goals.

✔ You stay present to money truths. You are aware of the possibility of money fantasies running your life. You recognize them and let them go, choosing instead to live in money truth.

Path One:
Self-referencing
and Conscious
Choice

In youth we learn.
In age we understand.

— Ella Wheeler-Wilcox

You are ready to be responsible and conscious about money. This path includes a look at your existing money patterns, habits, conversations and beliefs. Some of these beliefs are conscious, some unconscious.

Unconscious beliefs are patterns of which you are unaware and which appear unknowable. So how are you going to access them? Two ways. First you are going to look at your past. Key life events give you clues, which you can patch together to identify your money fantasies.

Second, you are going to look at your present results. Your results stem from your intentions. When your intentions are unconscious, looking at your results can bring them into focus.

First let's investigate your money history. Before you begin, take care of any details that may get in your way. Turn off the TV and find a quiet place. Tell your family not to disturb you. Get yourself a cup of tea or a glass of water. Prepare to be self-sufficient.

Set aside at least thirty minutes. The complete exercise will take about an hour and a half to two hours, but I suggest you do it in thirty-minute segments to allow yourself some processing time in between. When you begin again, start by reviewing what you wrote in the last session. You may also choose to do this exercise all at once. Choose whatever works for you. There is no right or wrong way.

Before you begin, take a few minutes to close your eyes and get centered. Calm the voices in your head.

Prosperity Insight

If you are in a committed partnership, share this work with your partner. First do the exercises on your own. Then set up a time to disclose your answers to your partner. Before you share, set boundaries. It is important not to judge, just to be present and listen. Take each question, and just listen to each other. To facilitate listening, simply repeat back to your partner what he or she says. Do not editorialize or comment.

This non-judgmental sharing looks something like this:

Partner:
When I was growing up my mother took care of all the money in my household.

Partner response:
When you were growing up your mother took care of all the money in your household.

Notice there is no commentary or judgment. Just repeat back what your partner says. This way your partner feels validated and listened to. The person speaking feels heard. The partner listening can listen rather than think about his or her response. The listening partner must also listen intently; this practice alone eliminates the self-talk in one's head. Everybody wins.

Ask them to take a break so you can focus on the task at hand. Center yourself by breathing deeply and focusing on the feel of the air as deep in your belly as you can breathe. If you practice meditation, you can use those skills here.

Do not begin the exercises until you have quieted your mind. When you are calm and ready to be self-reflective, answer the following questions. If you find you just can't get quiet today, give yourself permission to simply read through the questions, and choose another time to answer them.

If you are not in a committed relationship, find someone in your community to be your partner for this purpose. Because you have been taught to keep your money life secret, the simple act of sharing is healing on its own. Self-disclosing is a powerful way to transform your money life.

Answer the following questions about money from your childhood:

Growing up

What was money like when you were growing up? Look at your early childhood, your adolescence, your life as a teen and your early adult life.

Who controlled the money in your household? How did that person relate to money? What did that person believe about money?

_____

_____

_____

What did the parent who did not control the money in your household believe about money? How did he or she view money?

_____

_____

_____

Was there someone in your family or center of influence you admired because of his or her relationship to money? What did you admire?

_____

_____

_____

Was there harmony or argument around money?

_____

_____

_____

...About money from your childhood

How did your parents come to agreement about money?

_____

_____

_____

Was there an abundance? How did you know?

_____

_____

_____

Was there limitation? How did you know?

_____

_____

_____

Describe the first time you were aware of the concept of money. What is your earliest memory of money?

_____

_____

_____

Did you get an allowance? What did you do with your allowance? Save it? Spend it? What did you spend it on? Yourself or others?

_____

_____

_____

...About money from your childhood

When did you begin work? Why did you want to work? What was
your motivation?

_____

_____

_____

How did you use this first self-generated money? Did you save it? Spend it? What did you
spend it on? Yourself or others?

_____

_____

_____

Did you relate differently to money you earned vs. money given to you?

_____

_____

_____

As a child how did you view money?

_____

_____

_____

What event(s) or conversations about money do you remember vividly
from your childhood?

_____

_____

_____

...About money from your childhood

Do you have a money memory that you find painful to recall?

_____

_____

_____

Once you have answered all these questions, find the patterns or recurring themes.

What money fantasies do you see in your answers?

_____

_____

_____

_____

_____

_____

_____

_____

_____

_____

_____

_____

_____

_____

Prosperity Fable

At a seminar on *Changing your Relationship to Money* the group broke down in pairs to complete this exercise. I partnered with Susan, and as she shared her answers with me the patterns were illuminated. When discussing her earliest memories of money she told me that her mother kept money hidden from her dad. She knew there was limitation in her home because her mother often told her she could not have things she wanted, yet she bought things for herself with money she kept concealed. Her earliest money memory was her older brother taking her shopping. He bought Susan new clothes, but he made her promise not to tell her parents about the shopping trip or what things cost. With each question the theme of money secrets unfolded. Susan had been taught that you keep your money a secret; you hide it even from your life partner. The other message was it is acceptable to indulge yourself if you do so in secret!

Write a sentence of gratitude about each past money fantasty. Follow each gratitude sentence with one releasing this old belief into the universe. Lastly complete the work with a statement of acceptance of your new belief.

It might look something like this:

In the past I have believed that wealthy people were mean and hurtful. That it was impossible to be both wealthy and good. I appreciate this belief and express gratitude for the many blessings it has manifested in my life. I release this belief to its proper place in the universe. I accept the new belief that a wealthy person can be loving and truly good.

_____

_____

_____

_____

_____

_____

Personal Insight

Growing up, my family was middle class. We lived in a small town where most people knew each other. I saw my parents interact with people of all economic levels. When my father was around people of affluence he would become cautious and reserved. I often heard him say that if you are wealthy, you can hurt other people and there is no justice. As I looked at my own reactions to those of means, I realized that just like my dad, I felt fear. As part of my journey was live in Truth, I deliberately chose to put myself in situations where I would meet wealthy people. To be present to who they really were rather than reacting from my own learned filter. This discovery and letting go was critical to my own prosperity thinking. As long as I held onto my dad's view, that wealthy people hurt others without justice, I would never be able to achieve wealth because it was in conflict with being good.

Over the next few weeks, be particularly self-observant. Observe which limiting beliefs show up in your daily life. In your meditation practice, bring your awareness to your beliefs and ask for guidance on release. With each observation, prepare gratitude and release statements. Read your gratitude and release statements daily for twenty-one days.

My experience has been that when I work with clients who are truly committed to changing their relationship to money, everything in their lives that does not work about money will show up. It may seem as if your money challenges are on loudspeaker. This is just your old pattern making its last claim on you before you let it go. Do not waver in your commitment to change. Step into faith. Know that you can be the person you really desire to be around money. Do not give in to your tendency to get discouraged. Do not give up. Change takes patience, practice and self-care.

As you are practicing self-observation, continue your discovery process by exploring your present attitudes and feelings about money. Notice if there are similarities in your past money patterns and your current reality. Be brutally honest with your answers.

Answer the following questions about your present results around money:

Present results

How do you feel, what are your emotions about money?

When you are in abundance?

_____

_____

_____

When you have limitations?

_____

_____

_____

When there is enough? That is, you have enough without it being abundant or insufficient?

_____

_____

_____

The action of spending money gives us all something. What is that for you?

_____

_____

_____

...Present results around money

The action of saving money gives us all something. What is that for you?

_____

_____

_____

Accumulating money in the form of assets gives us all something. What is that for you?

_____

_____

_____

What is your favorite activity around money? Does spending, saving, or reflecting on what you have accumulated bring you the most pleasure?

_____

_____

_____

Do you see any ways in which your childhood and your present are similar around money?

_____

_____

_____

Where in your life are your past money patterns still present?

_____

_____

_____

...Present results around money

Notice what you have discovered. Write a statement about the present condition of your money life.

_____

_____

_____

Now that you have looked at your present actions and feelings around money, do you see any more fantasies you are holding on to?

_____

_____

_____

Write a sentence of gratitude and release for these past money fantasies just as you did previously.

_____

_____

_____

Now that you're complete with your money past and present, see a new intention for your money life in the future. For example, It is my intention to be conscious and prosperous in my money life. *Write your intention statement here:*

_____

_____

_____

_____

_____

_____

Symbols

Before leaving this investigation into your money fantasies, explore what money represents for you. Remember Truth Five about money: It is a creation of humankind, a form of energy and has value because we agree.

Answer the following questions about your money symbols:

What need in your life have you used money to fill?

_____

_____

What desires do you have that you perceive money fulfills?

_____

_____

What is money a symbol of for you? What does it represent in your life? What does it provide?

_____

_____

There are usually just a handful of things money ultimately represents for people. Answers are often things like, choices, security, freedom, joy, fun, and safety. There is no correct answer. You will probably also find that your answer is different from your partner. There are no right or wrong answers. You are simply uncovering your dreams.

Is the symbol or representation you currently hold about money limiting you? Or is it progressing your movement to The Intersection of Joy and Money?

_____

_____

_____

Intention and Result Exercise

You may be complete in your journey of self-discovery at this point. If you are then there is no need to complete the next set of exercises. Instead, skip over to the conclusion of Chapter Six. If you feel there is more to uncover, another tactic to find them is to look at your current results.

Make a list of the outcomes or results presently in your life around money. These are the financial consequences of your life. First just list them. For example, I have $10,000 in credit card debt. I make $50,000 a year. I save three hundred dollars a month. I fear running out of money. I feel poor. I worry about money. I understand how money works in my life. I let other people take care of me around money. Write down whatever is true.

Personal Insight

For me, money has always been a symbol of security. Prior to unwinding my money past, I believed that if I saved enough money, I would be safe. Now I experience my security from within. I know that nothing outside myself could ever provide safety. I still have a regular savings plan, but I now view my savings as giving me options. With money in savings, I have choices. I have taken time off, altered my career focus, and started several new businesses — all things I was able to give to myself because I had a savings plan. Notice that if I had held tightly onto the notion that money was security, I would not have been able to give myself permission to spend a portion of my savings on my new future. You would not be reading this book, as I would not have taken the liberty to write it!

Write your list of present results of your money life here:

▪ _____

▪ _____

▪ _____

▪ _____

▪ _____

▪ _____

Prosperity Insight

In a world without purpose, without meaningful values, what have we to share but our emptiness, the needy fragments of our superficial selves?

As a result, most of us scramble about hungrily seeking distraction, in music, in television, in people, in drugs.

Most of all we seek things.

Things to wear and things to do.

Things to fill up the emptiness.

Things to shore up our eroding sense of self.

Things to which we can attach meaning, significance, life.

We've fast become a world of things. And most people are being buried in the profusion.

Michael Gerber
The E-Myth Revisited

In the next section, re-write your results and comlete the intention and feeling exercise. First, repeat the result. Second, write your intention, as follows. Begin each statement with the words *I intend to be*_____.
For example, instead of writing *I have $10,000 in credit card debt*, write, *I intend to have $10,000 in credit card debt.* Next, be present to these intentions. Spend time with the feeling of each one. How does it feel to have $10,000 in credit card debt? Where does that feeling reside in your body? How much energy do you spend daily to keep that feeling unconscious?

Write down the feelings and where they reside in your body in the next section. Stay present to the feeling. The feeling will not last forever. It is only a feeling. It is not who you are. Resist the urge to stuff the feeling back into your unconsciousness. Let it make a complete cycle by coming up and fully dissipating on its own. This may take minutes. This may take days, weeks or months. Until the feeling runs its course, you are not complete with this result and ready to shift this intention. Continue to complete the "intentions-equal-results" exercises. Also continue to work through the remaining material. Keep feeling those unprocessed emotions as you complete the remaining exercises in this workbook.

Let's look at an example: Your credit card debt makes you feel embarrassed and ashamed. Stay with these feelings. If you practice meditation, set your intention before meditation to transform these feelings. Share them with your partner. Cry if you feel like it. Yell if you feel like it. Hit a pillow. Whatever helps you feel the feeling, do it.

Notice when the feeling shifts. Stay with the feeling until it runs its course naturally. At some point the embarrassed and ashamed feelings will melt away into a desire for change. You will experience a drive to do what it takes to alter your behavior around credit card debt. Lastly, with your feelings complete, now you are ready. Write down your new intention. Write down your new attitude. Write a sentence that says in present tense your future intention. Do not use negatives in these sentences in any way.

For example, *It is my intention to be credit card debt free. I will do what it takes to manifest my intention.*

Do not say, *I am not in credit card debt.*

Go back to your list of results. For each one individually, write it down, with your current intentions, followed by your feelings and new intentions and affirmations in this section:

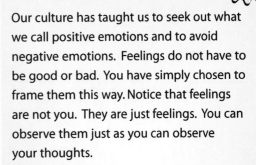

Prosperity Insight

Our culture has taught us to seek out what we call positive emotions and to avoid negative emotions. Feelings do not have to be good or bad. You have simply chosen to frame them this way. Notice that feelings are not you. They are just feelings. You can observe them just as you can observe your thoughts.

When you evade negative emotions you do so by suppressing them. It feels yucky and you want the feeling to go away. Rather than detaching from the feeling and allowing it to run its normal cycle, you resist it and push it away. This allows the feeling to stay stuck in your body. To hold it down, to keep it away, you have to continue to give it energy. By bringing it back into consciousness and allowing it to process, you free up the energy you were using on suppression.

...Intention and result exercise

Result

_____

_____

Intention

_____

_____

Feelings and where they reside in your body

_____

_____

New intention and affirmation

_____

_____

Result

_____

_____

Intention

_____

_____

Feelings and where they reside in your body

_____

_____

New intention and affirmation

_____

_____

...Intention and result exercise

Result

_____

_____

Intention

_____

_____

Feelings and where they reside in your body

_____

_____

New intention and affirmation

_____

_____

Result

_____

_____

Intention

_____

_____

Feelings and where they reside in your body

_____

_____

New intention and affirmation

_____

_____

…Intention and result exercise

Result

_____

_____

Intention

_____

_____

Feelings and where they reside in your body

_____

_____

New intention and affirmation

_____

_____

Result

_____

_____

Intention

_____

_____

Feelings and where they reside in your body

_____

_____

New intention and affirmation

_____

_____

...Intention and result exercise

Result

_____

_____

Intention

_____

_____

Feelings and where they reside in your body

_____

_____

New intention and affirmation

_____

_____

Result

_____

_____

Intention

_____

_____

Feelings and where they reside in your body

_____

_____

New intention and affirmation

_____

_____

...Intention and result exercise

Result

_____

_____

Intention

_____

_____

Feelings and where they reside in your body

_____

_____

New intention and affirmation

_____

_____

Result

_____

_____

Intention

_____

_____

Feelings and where they reside in your body

_____

_____

New intention and affirmation

_____

_____

...Intention and result exercise

Result

_____

_____

Intention

_____

_____

Feelings and where they reside in your body

_____

_____

New intention and affirmation

_____

_____

Result

_____

_____

Intention

_____

_____

Feelings and where they reside in your body

_____

_____

New intention and affirmation

_____

_____

Your new intentions are now in the form of affirmations. Use the worksheet on page 107 to re-state your affirmations. Take these affirmations and refer to them once or twice a day. Read them silently. Read them aloud. Read them to your partner and in front of a mirror. Say the statements as if you mean them. Notice the feeling in your body when you say the affirmations. For now, don't struggle to make them true. Just affirm that they are true.

If your partner is not open to listening or working with you on this exercise, share with a good friend. This is your transformation. Don't rob yourself of your new life by waiting for someone else's approval or participation.

> *Letting go of your past creates a vacuum for new ideas and ways of thinking to come into your life.*

The exercises in the rest of this book will help you bring these affirmations into truth. Affirmations by themselves will not create a new money life for you. It takes action. As you work through the rest of the exercises, you will see how to take action that is congruent with your goals.

The purpose of this work is to create a new relationship for you and money. The goal is to create lasting change, or transformation, in your money life. By illuminating your past, you can choose to let it go. Before you can take in new ideas, you have to release old ones. Letting go of your past creates a vacuum for new ideas and ways of thinking to come into your life. These new ideas form the foundation of your money future.

Let's look at an example. Perhaps one of your old ideas is that someone else will provide for you

Prosperity Fable

Jeri had lived the first 45 years of her life just getting by financially. She hired me as her coach to change this pattern. We began by looking at her money fantasies. We uncovered several stories from her childhood, but one kept coming up as the most profound.

When she was twelve, her father required that she work during her summer break. Jeri wanted to have fun and play, but her father insisted she take a baby-sitting job. All summer she cared for three children, ages six, two and an infant. Her father was adamant that she save all her money. He took her to the local savings and loan and they opened her first savings account. Jeri consoled herself, that while she was not having fun like her friends, at least she would have a great deal of money to buy something special .

When school started in the fall, her father announced it was time to buy school clothes. Excited to go shopping, Jeri hopped in the car. Their first stop was the savings and loan, where her father withdrew all her summer earnings. He then used all her baby-sitting money to buy her new school clothes. Her excitement faded into unexpressed anger. As a child she was powerless to express the anger she felt.

As Jeri spent time with this story, she saw clearly that it was still haunting her. She was replaying several patterns from this story. She would work hard, get ahead and save money. Then each September, no matter the circumstance, she would find herself broke again just like when she was twelve.

She also saw a destructive pattern in her work habits. Often when she needed to really focus on her business, she would have a temper tantrum and go play. Jeri was sabotaging the progress of her business with play. It was her way of masking the anger buried so long ago.

Now Jeri could see clearly that the only person she was hurting was herself. Present to this story, and its lingering effects on her life, Jeri moved forward to uncover her pain and release it from her body. She used cranio-sacral and traditional therapy to access the hidden feelings of powerlessness, betrayal and hurt. It took several months and many tears, but by allowing these old hurts to be felt she could release them and let them go. As the buried feelings left her body, she was free from her own trap. Reclaiming her own power, she moved forward to expand her business and her net worth.

financially. You see this pattern in your parents' roles, in the ways you were taught to think of money as a child, and in your early relationships. You now see that in giving your responsibility away you give your power away. You want to choose again.

So how might you go about this? Knowing the four steps of transformation, first realize you just moved from Step One, Unconscious Incompetence, to Step Two, Conscious Incompetence. You are not any better at being responsible for yourself financially than you were a few minutes ago. All you have done is realize you want to change.

> *Remember to reach out to your community. It is human to need support to change.*

To get to Step Three, Conscious Competence, begin by becoming an observer of your own behavior. Notice your language, your actions, and your thoughts and how they support the belief that someone else provides for you. Each time you notice, you can choose again. At first you may find you notice after one or two days, or a week, following an event. You may have a tendency to beat yourself up because you continued to act on your old patterns. Do just the contrary. This is the time to celebrate. The good news is you noticed.

As you continue to observe your own thoughts, feelings and actions, you will notice the change cycle accelerate. Each opportunity brings more awareness. You are continuing to grow in your understanding of how much you have been on autopilot.

Now you can choose again by slowing down in your responses. Pause and see if this is really how you want to react before you do so. Keep up your awareness and before long you will be at Step Four, Unconscious Competence. You will now choose thoughts, words and deeds that represent the new you — the you responsible for your own financial future.

Begin to notice how your old rules are manifested in your life. Listen to your self-talk. Watch your behavior. You may again find journaling helpful at this step. Change can be challenging and scary. Remember to reach out to your community. It is human to need support to change. Give yourself permission to allow your transformation to look like whatever it looks like. Let go of self-judgment and be fully present to the journey. ■

Summary

- ✓ Your personal money fantasies are hidden in your past.

- ✓ Find your fantasies, feel the feelings long buried, and release them.

- ✓ Releasing your past frees you to create a new money future.

- ✓ Repeat your new intentions and affirmations for your money life daily for twenty-one days.

My Affirmations

- _____
_____

- _____
_____

- _____
_____

- _____
_____

- _____
_____

- _____
_____

- _____
_____

- _____
_____

- _____
_____

- _____
_____

- _____
_____

7

Path Two:
Responsibility
and **Reality**

It isn't where you come from;
it's where you're going that counts.

— Ella Fitzgerald

The next part of the journey is to bring responsibility and reality into your relationship with money. You may continue to work through the Chapter Six exercises as well. It is necessary for you to uncover your money history and patterns, but it is not required that you complete this prior to bringing in responsibility and reality.

There are two steps to responsibility and reality: one, identifying your financial position; and two, clearly looking at your cash flow.

Your financial position is simply an inventory of your assets and liabilities at a point in time. Your assets are things that you own of value. Your liabilities are debts or obligations you must satisfy in the future. Examples of assets are your home, stocks, bonds, real estate, collectables, and business interests. Examples of liabilities are your mortgage, credit card balances, car loans, and unpaid taxes.

Determine your financial position using the worksheet in Appendix A. Begin by distinguishing investment assets and liabilities from lifestyle assets and liabilities. Investment assets are those that send you a check; you may also expect them to have more value in the future. These are assets which generate cash flow you can use to support your lifestyle. This includes certificates of deposit, stocks, bonds, a closely held business and rental real estate. These assets may be inside a retirement plan, such as a 401(k), company pension or IRA or held personally. If they are held in a retirement plan they are tax-deferred assets, that is, the earnings grow sheltered from current income tax. If they are held outside a retirement plan, they are after-tax assets, and the income is generally taxable.

Lifestyle assets are assets you choose to have in your life for your pleasure and enjoyment. These assets do not send you a check and generally require that you spend money maintaining and insuring them. You do not intend to use the proceeds or cash flow from these assets to support your lifestyle. These include assets such as your home, vacation home, car, jewelry, or gun collection.

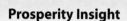

Prosperity Insight

Preparing a Statement of Financial Position annually is a great way to stay responsible and conscious with money. It also gives you a concrete way to observe your net worth increase and celebrate your achievement.

List each asset at its fair market value. That is what a willing buyer and seller would exchange this asset for, where neither is under the compulsion to buy or sell. In other words, what you believe you could get in cash for this asset if you were selling it in the ordinary course of life. List the total fair market value. You will list the liability in that section of the worksheet.

Next list your liabilities. These are any and all debts that you have. List each one and its current balance, that is, the lump sum of money required to pay the debt in full. Group your liabilities into the same categories as your assets, investment and lifestyle. If the liability was used to acquire an investment asset, it is an investment debt. If the liability was used to acquire a lifestyle asset, it is a lifestyle debt.

Investment liabilities are generally those where the asset you acquired is intended to service the debt. Examples are mortgages on rental property and margin loans on your portfolio.

Prosperity Fable

Karen and Jack were close to seventy. Jack had spent his working life with the U.S. government and was planning to retire on his government pension. He and Karen had about $60,000 saved as an additional nest egg, in certificates of deposit (CDs) in a local bank. They had never invested in the stock market.

Jack's best friend Lee was dying of cancer. Lee was a self-made businessman, and had saved for his own retirement investing in stocks. Lee encouraged Jack to do a favor for another friend who was new in the investment business by turning his CDs over to him. Jack felt Lee knew more than he did, so as the CDs matured he took Lee's broker's advice and invested in something he called foreign trades. Thirty days later, Jack received a letter saying all his money was lost. There were no foreign trades. Rather the broker had absconded with the money.

Jack had fallen into several easy traps. One, assuming others know more than you. Two, basing a decision on friendship rather than doing your homework. Three, investing in something you do not understand.

Your lifestyle assets generally secure lifestyle liabilities. Examples are home mortgage, credit card debt, and auto loans.

Insert totals where noted on the worksheet. Do the same for your liabilities. Compute the net equity in each classification. Take your investment assets and deduct your investment liabilities to determine your investment net worth. Do the same for your lifestyle assets. Lastly compute a percentage of your net worth in each classification.

Review the example on the following pages before completing your State of Financial Condition using the appendix A worksheet.

Example:
Bill and Mary Jones
Statement of Financial Position

As of (date) December 31, 2002

Lifestyle assets:

Personal residence: $ 150,000

Automobiles:

Chevy $ 7,800

Toyota $ 12,500

Collectables:

Figurines $ 3,500

Coins $ 1,200

Household:

Furnishings $ 25,000

Other:

Jewelry $ 2,000

Total fair market value of lifestyle assets: $ 202,000

...Statement of financial position

Lifestyle liabilities:

Personal residence mortgage: $ 103,000

Automobile loans:

    Toyota $ 14,000

Credit card debt:

    Visa $ 3,000

    Department Store $ 1,800

Other:

    Due to Parents (home down payment) $ 7,500

Total obligations of lifestyle liabilities: $ 129,300

Net worth, lifestyle: $ 72,700

(Assets minus liabilities)

Investment assets:

After tax assets:

Checking accounts:

    FNB Bank $ 1,200

Savings accounts:

    Today's S&L $ 2,700

Certificates of deposit:

    First Union $ 5,200

...Statement of financial position

Money market accounts:

Schwab $ 1,600

Mutual funds:

Vanguard (various funds) $ 23,400

Fidelity (various funds) $ 9,900

Individually held stocks or securities:

Microsoft $ 5,270

Coca-Cola $ 4,830

Rental real estate:

2824 Stanley Lane $ 90,000

Business or professional practice:

M&S Associates, 50% interest $ 75,000

Other:

Bill's IRA $ 18,300

Mary's IRA $ 26,100

Tax-deferred accounts:

IRA:

Bill $ 82,650

Mary $ 138,700

Other:

SIMPLE $ 12,350

Total investment assets: $ 497,200

...Statement of financial position

Investment liabilities:

Mortgages, rental property:

    __2824 Stanley Lane__ $_____62,100_____

Loans to acquire business interests:

    __M&S Associates__ $_____55,000_____

Total obligations of investment liabilities: $_____117,100_____

Investment Net Worth: $_____380,100_____
(Assets minus liabilities)

Total net worth, investment and lifestyle: $_____452,800_____

Percentage of net worth, lifestyle: _____83.9_____%

Percentage of net worth, investment: _____16.1_____%

                                                    _100%_

Cash flow analysis

Next let's look at your present relationship to money in action by looking at your cash flow. The way money flows in and out of your life is a moment-to-moment representation of your patterns, beliefs, values and conversations about money. The more reality you bring in to your relationship with money, the closer you get to *The Intersection of Joy and Money.*

How do you analyze your cash flow?

I suggest you use a computerized checkbook manager program such as *Quicken*™ or *Microsoft Money*™. Alternatively you can use a computerized

...Statement of Financial Position

spreadsheet. Or if you really dislike computers altogether, an old fashioned columnar pad is a good start. The form really doesn't matter. What does matter is that you do the exercise.

For both your cash inflows and outflows, you will need to analyze transactions for a minimum of six months, although a year is better. Be as specific as possible and use as much detail as possible. If in doubt, use more rather than less categories. For example, separate dining out from groceries, rather than having one category named food. If you need to change your spending habits following the analysis, the more detail you have, the more clarity you will have regarding your options.

Let's begin by looking at your inflows. Use four broad categories to summarize your inflows. The broad categories are:

- Return on labor

- Return on assets

- Return on a combination of assets and labor

- Gifts

Return on labor is the cash flow you get from what we call *work*. If you have to put in time to get this cash flow, it is return on labor. In recording return on labor you will record it at gross. That is, you will record your gross pay as income, and all your withholdings as expenses.

This process alone may cause you a little anxiety. You may never have looked at how much of your

...Statement of Financial Position

income you contribute to causes such as the federal, state and local government. If you gain nothing else from this exercise, hopefully you will acquire a commitment to reduce your taxes with every means legally available to you.

Return on assets includes items such as interest and dividends. It is the category for all cash flow that comes in from your investment assets. Stocks, real estate, bonds, certificates of deposit, and closely held businesses are examples of assets that produce investment cash flow. Many of these assets you accumulated by investing a portion of your cash flow over time.

You may also have assets you created from your labor. For example, you may have written a book, published a training manual, developed a trademark process, and built a valuable closely held business with sweat equity, or you may own several rental properties where you have a property manager taking care of the day-to-day details. These assets at one time required your labor but now they do not. They have been converted from return on labor to return on assets because you no longer work to acquire their cash flows.

Return on a combination of assets and labor includes assets where the cash flow is not easily distinguished between return on labor and return on assets. It is helpful to differentiate this return, and I will speak to how to do this later. For now identify those assets where you have both a monetary investment and a labor investment. These are assets such as a closely held business that requires your services to be viable,

> *If you gain nothing else from this exercise, hopefully you will acquire a commitment to reduce your taxes...*

or rental real estate where you are the property manager. If you cannot take an extended vacation from the business or property, it requires your labor and is a mixed-return asset.

Gifts: This is self-explanatory. If you did not work for the money, and it is not from an asset, then you received a gift. In this category record all gifts.

As noted above you will be as detailed as possible in your analysis. If you have two jobs in your household, you will have two categories for return on labor. If you have rental property and stocks, you will have two categories for return on assets. If in doubt be more detailed. You can always go back and subtotal your information if needed.

For a closely held business interest, or rental real estate, list the cash flow that is available to you personally. Do not list the gross receipts of these businesses and the related business expenses. In this exercise we are just focused on cash flow which is free for your personal use.

When complete, compute the percentage inflow from each category, return on labor, return on assets, return on combination of assets and labor, and gifts. For example, if your total cash inflows are $100,000, and your return on labor is $30,000, then your percentage inflow from return on labor is 30% (30,000/100,000).

Review the example on the following pages before completing your cash inflow analysis using the Appendix B worksheet.

Here is an outline to use for this purpose:
Bill and Mary Jones
Year ending December 31, 2002

Cash Inflows

Return on labor:

Gross pay __Bill__	$	47,000
Gross pay __Mary__	$	26,000
Total return on labor:	$	73,000 75.8%

Return on assets:

Stock dividends:	$	620
Interest earned:	$	280
Stock dividends and capital gains-IRA and 401(k)	$	8,300
Total return on assets:	$	9,200 9.6 %

Return on combination of assets and labor:

Closely held business:

S Corp distributions:	$	10,000
Rental property net cash flow:	$	2,550
Total mixed return cash flow:	$	12,550 13.0%

Gifts:

Source:

__Grandparents__	$	1,500
Total gifts:	$	1,500 1.6%
Total inflows, all sources:	$	96,250 100%

Let's go back to the topic of differentiating the return on labor and return on asset component of closely held business or personally owned rental real estate. In both these cases, you applied your expertise to the acquisition, building and maintenance of these assets. How much cash flow you take in the form of a paycheck and how much of the return is in the form of dividends or profit distributions is generally a tax-driven decision. That is, you take the return in the form that creates the least taxable income, as well you should.

The downside is that this creates a distorted picture of the true return from the asset. If you work outside a closely held business, your wages are determined in a negotiated, arm's-length transaction between yourself and your employer. For you to get a true picture of your efforts and return on labor, you need to apply the same arm's-length standard in analyzing your closely held interests in companies and real estate.

Here are a couple of examples. Let's say to hire a real-estate manager would cost you six percent of your gross rental income. You do not *pay yourself* this fee, because you own the property. But when analyzing how much money you are making from your true investment in real estate, and how much you are making as a return on labor, you should consider this a cost. For if you wanted the freedom to come and go as you please, you would need to hire a management company. So while this is not an incurred cost, it is an opportunity cost.

Looking at a closely held business you can apply the same result. What is a fair market value for the services you render to your company? That is, what would you pay someone to do your job? It may be more or less than you actually take in your paycheck. This true arm's-length wage is an opportunity cost for you. For you to have freedom with your time, for your return to be just from your investment, you would have to incur this cost. Looking at your business this way will give you a clearer, more realistic picture of how it is working for you.

Cash flow analysis, outflow

Now let's look at your cash outflows. Summarize your outflows using the Appendix C worksheet into the following categories:

- Taxes (all taxes, property, income, social security, state, local)

- Savings, pre-tax

- Savings, post-tax

- Debt payments, interest and principal

- Insurance, all types, health, disability, etc.

- Costs of your home, excluding debt

- Other spending, necessities

- Other spending, wants

Be very detailed in your categories. You can always go back and take out details, but it is time-consuming to do the reverse. Once you have completed the analysis, compute the percentage spending in each broad category using the space provided. For example, if your total cash outflows are $80,000, and your debt payments, interest and principal are $15,000, then the percentage for this category is 18.75% (15,000/80,000).

Review the example on the next page before completing your cash outflow analysis using the Appendix C worksheet. If you are using a computerized program, set up the system using the Appendix C categories.

Complete your summary for at least six months, preferably a year. Then compute the percentage of income you spend in each major classification.

The discernment of wants and necessities is somewhat ambiguous. For example, you need reliable transportation to get to and from work. An economy car is a necessity. But suppose you want a luxury car. So part of this cash flow out is a need and a part is a want. This will be the case in many areas. For now, differentiate between wants and needs as best you can. Your value system may categorize wants and needs differently than is above. Use what feels right to you. For example, massage may be a want or a need. It may be determined by your point of view, or it may be determined by your medical history. If a prior back injury keeps you in ill health without a massage, it is a need. There is no right or wrong, just discern what feels true for you. We will revisit this area following the next chapter on goals and strategies.

Bill and Mary Jones
As of (date) _Year ending December 31, 2002_

Cash flow analysis, out flow

Taxes:

Federal income tax:	$ 13,900	
State income tax:	$ 4,100	
Local income tax:	$ 520	
Social Security tax:	$ 4,526	
Medicare tax:	$ 1,095	
Real estate tax:	$ 1,500	
Personal property tax:	$ 229	
Total taxes:	$ 25,870	27.1%

Savings, pre-tax:

Stock dividends inside, IRA & 401(k)	$ 8,300	
401(k)	$ 3,700	
SIMPLE	$ 3,000	
	$ 15,000	15.6%

Savings, after tax: $ 700 .1%

...Bill and Mary Jones example

Debt payments, principal and interest:

Deerfield S&L	$	8,200
Toyota loan	$	4,560
VISA	$	900
Department store	$	1,200
Loan from parents	$	500

Total debt payments: $ 15,360   16.1%

Insurance:

Health:	$	900
Life:	$	540
Disability:	$	650
Homeowners:	$	770
Automobile:	$	980

Total insurance: $ 3,840   4.1 %

Cost of primary home:

Utilities:	$	960
Cable TV:	$	540
Telephone:	$	660
Repairs and maintenance:	$	820
Improvements:	$	1,750
Internet service:	$	300
Furnishings:	$	620
Water and sewer:	$	240
Other:	$	190

Total costs of home: $ 6,080   6.3 %
(excluding mortgage and insurance)

...Bill and Mary Jones example

Other spending, necessity:

Automobile:

Gas:	$ 1,920
Repairs:	$ 1,400
Maintenance:	$ 480
Groceries:	$ 5,150

Health care:

Dental:	$ 240
Chiropractic:	$ 150
Physician:	$ 90
Pharmacy:	$ 240
Therapy:	$ 480
Gym:	$ 660
Massage:	$ 720

Education:

Tuition:	$ 1,500
Charitable giving:	$ 1,630
Total spending, necessity:	$ 14,660 15.3 %

...Bill and Mary Jones example

Other spending, wants:

       Cash, unidentified: $ 2,670

       Clothing: $ 3,300

Travel:

       Other: **Annual vacation** $ 2,200

Personal care:

       Hair care: $ 1,350

       Cosmetics: $ 280

Leisure:

       Books and magazines: $ 50

       Sporting events: $ 220

       Movies and video rental: $ 370

       Dining out: $ 1,440

       Entertaining: $ 600

       Sporting goods: $ 620

       Gifts: $ 1,240

       Other: $ 400

Total spending, wants: $ 14,740   15.4 %

Total spending: $ 96,250   100 %

Review your cash flow summary and ask yourself the following questions. Write down your response without judging yourself.

Reflections on financial position and cashflow exercise

Are you surprised by where your money really goes?

_____

_____

Where do you spend more than you thought?

_____

_____

Where do you spend less than you thought?

_____

_____

Do you see any spending patterns that do not support you?

_____

_____

How is your cash flow lined up with your past conversations about money?

_____

_____

What choices are you making about how you receive and spend money?

_____

_____

...Reflections on financial position

How do you intend to change those choices in the future?

_____

_____

What actions are needed to create change in your patterns of receiving and spending money?

_____

_____

_____

You may find it helpful to go back and review or re-answer the money history questions. See if you can find the connection between your personal money fantasies and your present patterns of receiving and spending money.

Keep this information, and continue to update it as you work in the next section on goals and strategies. ■

Prosperity Fable

Mr. and Mrs. Montgomery were retiring in six months. Their six children were grown and they were ready for new challenges. While they had managed to save a significant amount of money inside a company pension plan, they also had significant debts. They had always been told it was best to be debt free at retirement. Fortunately they came in to do some financial planning, primarily to discover the best way to service their debts, and make their pile last the rest of their lives.

I ran the numbers both ways, first by taking a distribution out of their retirement assets large enough to pay all their debts off, and second by consolidating their debt into a second mortgage line of credit that they would repay over seven years. The financial analysis showed clearly that consolidating their debt was the best alternative. If they tried to pay all their debt off in one lump sum, there just was not enough money left to support them through their retirement. The Montgomerys learned another valuable lesson; it pays to look specifically at your personal circumstances and to run the numbers!

Summary

To be responsible and to be in reality with money requires that:

- ✔ You know your financial position.
- ✔ You have clarity around the source of your cash flow.
- ✔ You consciously choose your cash out flow.

Chapter

8

PathThree:
Goals and **Strategies**

*What is very difficult at first,
if we keep trying, gradually
becomes easier.*

— Helen Keller

*I*n this section the terms *Goals* and *Strategies* may be used differently than you have used them previously. *Goals* are defined as the purpose, or source of your wants. *Strategies* are defined as the choices available to manifest your goals. Goals are feeling-based and have many paths to reach them. Strategies are desires or dreams with many possible results.

For example, you may want a new car. You have driven your neighbor's new car and it was a rush. It makes you feel young and pampered. The source of your desire, that is, your goal, is the feeling of being young and pampered. The strategy to *feeling young* is to get the car.

You know you have articulated your goal when you express your desire and it is an end point. It cannot be further articulated. To distinguish a goal from a strategy take your desires and ask, *What does this provide?* Continue to ask this question. When there isn't another answer, you have reached your goal.

Let's look at the example in the Prosperity Fable on page 136.

Notice that the process is simply to keep looking until there is no other answer. Look at what is provided from every response.

The question, *What does this provide?* may not resonate for you. If not, alternative questions are *What is the purpose of this?* or *What is the value of this?* Use the language you find most helpful. The purpose of the question is to get you to the deeper source of your desires. The form of getting there is only incidental to the outcome.

Prosperity Fable

Janice is working with her financial planner and tells her she wants to be financially independent at age fifty.

Planner:
What does being financially independent at age fifty provide?

Janice:
I never have to go to work again!

Planner:
What does not going to work ever again provide?

Janice:
I can explore all the hobbies I always wanted to, but never had time for.

Planner:
What does exploring hobbies provide?

Janice:
I always wondered if I was creative. I want to explore that part of myself and find out.

Planner:
What does getting in touch with your creativity provide?

Janice:
Access to the divine.

Planner:
What does access to the divine provide?

Janice:
Access to the divine.

For Janice this was her goal. Access to the divine was what she was seeking. It is both the source of her desires, and her desired outcome.

As you do this next exercise, say what comes up for you in each answer. Do not judge it, or hold back your first response. Write down the first thing that comes into your head.

Each of us is unique. Discovering your goals will yield answers that may vary from the example, your spouse, your neighbor or your best friend. Your goal may be to have more fun. Your goal may be to experience freedom. In your individuality you have your own way of expressing and your own dreams.

When you finish the goal and strategy exercise completely you will have only a handful of goals. If you have more than a few, review each, asking again, *What does this provide?* You will find there are only two to three core goals. You may have only one.

Begin by writing your *financial wants and desires* on the lines marked *Strategy*. First write down everything that comes to mind: a new home, your own business, early retirement, a college education for your children, security for your family in case of your premature death. Do not judge it or decide it is not achievable. Write down what occurs to you in the moment. Next take each strategy and ask the question, *What does this provide?* until there is no further answer.

Review the example that follows, then complete your own worksheet on page 139. Notice that there are two columns which say *provide*. In the center column list the first things that come to mind. In the column on the far right list your ultimate goal.

Personal Insight

My primary goal is joy. To keep myself focused, I have a mental exercise I go through when choosing what I want. I ask: *Does this access joy?* To choose otherwise is self-defeating. In the past I would often take on roles inside my company that did not serve me. These roles needed to be done, and rather than ask someone else to take them on, I had a handful of convenient reasons why it had to be me. Some of my best reasons were, *I can't ask _____ to do this; she is too busy. I can do this in 15 minutes; it would take me that long to delegate it. Only I can do this the way I want it done.* The truth was I was uncomfortable asking for what I needed. As a consequence instead of joy, I frequently found myself working late and being resentful. I had to learn to give up the reasons and stay committed to my chosen result, joy. What I discovered in this process is that when I truly asked for what I needed, it was provided without exception.

...Discover your goals sample worksheet

Strategy	Provides	Provides
House	Maintenance of property	FULL HEARTED JOY
Fix chimney	Wholeness in self	FULL HEARTED JOY
Fix front steps	Foundation to generate from	FULL HEARTED JOY
Gutter guards	Ability to expand	FULL HEARTED JOY
New kitchen floors	Getting destiny out	FULL HEARTED JOY
Wood floors refinished	Transformation on the planet	FULL HEARTED JOY
New garage Door	Exciting and peaceful	FULL HEARTED JOY
Dental work	Health	FULL HEARTED JOY
Weekly bodywork	Rejuvenation	FULL HEARTED JOY
	Ongoing transformation	
New Clothes	Framing of self	FULL HEARTED JOY
Consistently	Appreciation	
	Honoring new person	
	Adorning of self	
New car	Getting around	FULL HEARTED JOY
Travel	Exploration/rest	FULL HEARTED JOY
Training	Expansion of self	FULL HEARTED JOY
Great relationship	Satisfaction	FULL HEARTED JOY
	Partnership	
	Growth/development	
	Sex	
Healthy animals	Companionship	FULL HEARTED JOY
Writing	New paradigm	FULL HEARTED JOY

…Discovering your goals

Strategy	Provides	Provides
_____	_____	_____
_____	_____	_____
_____	_____	_____
_____	_____	_____
_____	_____	_____
_____	_____	_____
_____	_____	_____
_____	_____	_____
_____	_____	_____
_____	_____	_____
_____	_____	_____
_____	_____	_____
_____	_____	_____
_____	_____	_____
_____	_____	_____
_____	_____	_____
_____	_____	_____
_____	_____	_____
_____	_____	_____
_____	_____	_____
_____	_____	_____
_____	_____	_____
_____	_____	_____
_____	_____	_____

…Discovering your goals

Strategy	Provides	Provides
_____	_____	_____
_____	_____	_____
_____	_____	_____
_____	_____	_____
_____	_____	_____
_____	_____	_____
_____	_____	_____
_____	_____	_____
_____	_____	_____
_____	_____	_____
_____	_____	_____
_____	_____	_____
_____	_____	_____
_____	_____	_____
_____	_____	_____
_____	_____	_____
_____	_____	_____
_____	_____	_____
_____	_____	_____
_____	_____	_____
_____	_____	_____
_____	_____	_____
_____	_____	_____

…Discovering your goals

Strategy	Provides	Provides
_____	_____	_____
_____	_____	_____
_____	_____	_____
_____	_____	_____
_____	_____	_____
_____	_____	_____
_____	_____	_____
_____	_____	_____
_____	_____	_____
_____	_____	_____
_____	_____	_____
_____	_____	_____
_____	_____	_____
_____	_____	_____
_____	_____	_____
_____	_____	_____
_____	_____	_____
_____	_____	_____
_____	_____	_____
_____	_____	_____
_____	_____	_____
_____	_____	_____
_____	_____	_____

Now that you have your goal, or short list of goals, you will find there are many ways to reach it. Whether your goal is to access the divine, experience freedom or have more fun, you will find scores of options to reach your goal(s). This is where you really begin to explore the opportunity of your life.

Consider all the possibilities in the present moment. Consider the goal, *access to the divine*. What are ways you access the divine? Your list might include painting, drawing, writing, walking in the woods, riding a horse, prayer, or meditation.

Consider the goal, *to have fun*. Your list might include hiking in the park, going to the movies, reading a good mystery novel, playing charades with your family, or reading jokes that give you a good deep belly laugh.

Whatever your goal, you will find many ways to create it in your life. Explore these possibilities by journaling, sharing with your partner, or by working with the community you have generated.

Remember, you get *things* because of what they provide. You get a new car because of the feeling you have when you drive it. You purchase a new house because of the feeling of having your own home, because of the joy that comes from having your own personal space. Once you begin to see that the things you have are there to produce the feelings you want, you can bypass the things and go right to the feelings.

> *Once you begin to see that the things you have are there to produce the feelings you want, you can bypass the things and go right to the feelings.*

A whole new set of choices opens up for you once you distinguish between goals and strategies. This is also the point at which life gets really simple. Once you have reduced your strategies to their essence, life is uncomplicated. You can make powerful choices that support your goals. Your goals serve as a blueprint or intention. It will be easy to distinguish those actions that support your goals, and those that do not.

Even as your life choices expand, your life becomes simpler. A true paradox. Usually we think of simplicity as keeping things small. Yet simple can be really big.

Part of the path to *The Intersection of Joy and Money* is learning that you have many choices to get what you really want. This is true abundance. In the process you get a simple, uncomplicated life.

Once you have worked through the exercise to discern your goals, you are ready for the next step. On page 147, make a list of at least ten things which bring each goal into your life, but which cost absolutely nothing, or almost nothing.

For example, say your goal is to experience freedom. Look to see where in your life you experience freedom now that doesn't cost anything. For example, you experience freedom when you are in nature. You experience freedom when you spend time alone with a good book. You experience freedom when you give yourself permission to do absolutely nothing you consider work, even if it is for fifteen minutes. You experience freedom when you listen to your favorite music. And so on. List ways you experience freedom that cost nothing, things that are simple and easily brought into your life.

Next is the fun part. Indulge in your top ten things frequently. Do it with the intention of living your goal(s). Using the above example, *you experience freedom when you listen to your favorite music,* bring this intention of freedom into your awareness as you turn on the music. Notice how you feel about yourself and your life.

Personal Insight

In my pursuit of joy, one of the items on my *doesn't cost you anything* list is dancing. I absolutely love to dance. Sometimes I turn on music and dance at home. There is also a weekly dance a short distance from my house, and while it is not completely free, it is very inexpensive. When I dance I experience joy. That night I go to bed with a full heart, grateful for such a simple and complete expression of my desires.

On page 148, make a second list of strategies to your goal(s) that do include money. Put the dollars required next to each. For the things you can afford now, do them without delay. See how that feels. Notice what it is like to get what you want. Notice that it doesn't take a lot of effort, only clarity about your goal(s).

For strategies that require more money, begin a savings plan to support those goals. As you start your savings plan, stay focused on your goal. As you begin to work your plan, choices that you did not dream of may become available to you. Keep an open mind and stay focused on your goal.

Let's look at another example. Say one of your fun strategies is to own a lake house. You know that in your area a lake house costs $100,000 and another $15,000 a year to maintain. Begin your savings plan.

Begin to look at strategies for how to increase your income to bring in an additional $15,000 a year to pay for the maintenance. Set your goal and get in action.

Begin your plan and work it. Notice what happens. You may find something better shows up. Perhaps as you are saving for a lake house, an opportunity to travel abroad presents itself. This is something you always wanted. It's fun. Ask yourself the question: Does this meet my goal of fun? If so be open to changing your position and going in a new direction. Your goal is fun, not the lake house. Stay focused on the goal. And take action toward the goal, not the strategy.

In your quest for a lake house, perhaps you have a friend who owns a lake house and has invited you on many occasions to come and use the house. So the lake house is already available to you, all you have to do is call your friend.

Be present to the abundance of ways to increase the fun in your life. Often all that is needed is to make it a priority. Maybe all that is missing is your decision to have more fun, and your commitment to that goal. Creation follows intentions that are in action. Now that your intentions are focused on your goal, it will be natural for new creations or options to come to light.

As you work through this area, keep a journal. Once you have clarified your goals, write them down and

Prosperity Insight

Do not read this insight until you have completed the exercise on distinguishing goals and strategies in Chapter Eight.

It is likely that you will find the goals you identified in Chapter Eight are the same as what money represents or symbolizes for you in Chapter Six. For example if money represents full-hearted joy to you, then most likely your goal is full-hearted joy.

Prosperity Fable

Kate and I were exploring the expansion of her business. She had been in business fifteen years. The company had never really taken off. Through our work together, she discovered that her goal was *access to the divine*. Kate soon realized her business was not in line with her goal. While it is a great product, it was just a way to make money, and not a fulfilling one. She set her intention for the perfect buyer to come to light and purchase her business. As Kate made her top ten list, she was aware that she really missed her artwork. As part of her assignment, to indulge in things that provide her goal and cost nothing, Kate began painting. Within a few weeks a guest in her home saw her work, and offered her a $1000 retainer to create a piece for her. At the same time, Kate began to get offers to purchase her business. In the last fifteen years she had never received an offer to buy her business. Now she received two in less than a week. When you focus on your goals, often what needs to shift in your life does so effortlessly.

refer to them often. Display them in a prominent place where you see them daily.

If you are in a study group in relationship to this material, share your insights and goals with your group. If you are in relationship, communicate this work with your partner.

Use this worksheet to write down the options for accomplishing your goals. Notice the example before completing your own worksheet.

Ways to Bring Full-Hearted Joy
That cost nothing

Nature

Fully present in conversation

Being in partnership

Creating

Accomplishments

Enrolling without attachments

Eating really good food

Seeing great art

Ways to Bring Full-Hearted Joy
That cost nothing

Worksheet

_____

_____

_____

_____

_____

_____

_____

_____

_____

...Strategies

Next list your strategies that do require money.

Strategies that reach my goal: Their cost:

_____ $_____

_____ $_____

_____ $_____

_____ $_____

_____ $_____

_____ $_____

_____ $_____

_____ $_____

_____ $_____

_____ $_____

_____ $_____

_____ $_____

_____ $_____

_____ $_____

_____ $_____

_____ $_____

_____ $_____

_____ $_____

_____ $_____

…Strategies

Sort through your list and do right away those that are immediately affordable. Next make a list of the priorities for the remaining strategies.

Priorities as of _____

   1. _____

   2. _____

   3. _____

   4. _____

   5. _____

   6. _____

   7. _____

   8. _____

   9. _____

 10. _____

 11. _____

 12. _____

 13. _____

 14. _____

 15. _____

 16. _____

 17. _____

 18. _____

 19. _____

 20. _____

…Strategies

Periodically revisit your priorities and see if they have shifted. If so use the following worksheets to list your new priorities.

Priorities as of _____

1. _____

2. _____

3. _____

4. _____

5. _____

6. _____

7. _____

8. _____

9. _____

10. _____

11. _____

12. _____

13. _____

14. _____

15. _____

16. _____

17. _____

18. _____

19. _____

20. _____

…Strategies

Periodically revisit your priorities and see if they have shifted. If so use the following worksheets to list your new priorities.

Priorities as of _____

1. _____

2. _____

3. _____

4. _____

5. _____

6. _____

7. _____

8. _____

9. _____

10. _____

11. _____

12. _____

13. _____

14. _____

15. _____

16. _____

17. _____

18. _____

19. _____

20. _____

Prosperity Fable

Susan told me she wanted a smaller home. After looking at what this provides, it came down to freedom. Another strategy of Susan's was to expand her business. After drilling down to the root of this strategy, freedom again surfaced. This was the result for all but one of her strategies.

Three months prior, Susan had articulated what money represented for her. Her answer was *freedom*. Using this simple process, you find a paradox. As you expand the possibilities of your money life, you receive laser-like clarity in getting what you really want.

Revisiting your goals and strategies from time to time will increase your awareness of the powerful choices you can make. Remember the paradox: As your life choices expand, your life becomes simpler, and the path to the *Intersection of Joy and Money* becomes more clear. This is true abundance. ■

Summary

✔ Goals are the purpose or source of your wants.

✔ Strategies are choices available to manifest your goal.

✔ Strategies are dreams with many results.

✔ The *Intersection of Joy and Money* is accessible by distinguishing goals and strategies.

✔ You can use your goals as a blueprint for life choices.

Chapter

9

Path Four: **Congruent Action:** Bringing It All Together

Failure is impossible.

— Susan B. Anthony

The last few chapters have taken you through a series of exercises to allow you to experience the first two money truths: One, *You are responsible for your money life,* and Two, *Your consciousness is required for money health.*

In the next two chapters, you will work with Truth Three, *Each piece of your money life gives you the whole,* and Truth Four, *Choice is the ultimate power.* Having built your foundation, you will use Truths Three and Four to align your money present and future by looking at each piece of your money life and making present-moment, conscious choices. Remember that for choice to truly be choice, it must be conscious, that is, not stemming from your past, your fantasies or your fears, and with complete reality about the sources of your choice.

The components of your money life are:

- Money habits of mind
- Goals and strategies
- Current cash flow
- Future cash flow
- Planning for big-ticket items
- Current net worth
- Liquidity
- Risk management
- Financial independence
- Estate planning

- Income tax planning

- College funding

- Investment planning and management

- Aligning work with your essence
  and passion

Your cash flow and financial position are maps of your past. Your goals and strategies are a blue print of your future. By doing this work you have given yourself sufficient information to use the power of choice to align your cash flow and financial position with your goals and strategies. This is the essence of Path Four, *Congruent Action.*

Begin your alignment process by first simply reviewing all the information you have gathered. Re-read your goals, strategies and priorities. Look over your cash flows and financial position. Do you see any obvious areas where you can realign effortlessly?

There may be some very simple choices that seemingly jump off the page. Pay particular attention to your goals. They are your focus.

Let's explore this idea. Say your goal is *freedom.* Look at your cash inflows and cash outflows and see if they are aligned with freedom. Perhaps you have over-extended yourself with a home that requires a large monthly mortgage payment, or you own an older home that requires constant maintenance. Does this home serve you in your pursuit of freedom? Are your actions in alignment with your goal?

Perhaps you have a high-paying job. You are a senior manager in your company. The standards of the company are a fifty to fifty-five hour workweek, and you spend an hour a day commuting. When you get home you are exhausted from the stress of the day and have difficulty enjoying your family. Your friends are few and far between, because you simply do not have time to spare. Does this accomplish your goal of freedom?

You will notice there is no right or wrong. All there is to do is to align your cash flows and financial position with your goals and strategies. How might you go about this?

Looking at the home example, an obvious choice might be to sell this home and buy a condo, a smaller home, or a newer home. Another option might be to hire a maintenance person to relieve you of the fix-it jobs.

Looking at the stressful job example, one apparent choice is to quit your job, find a less stressful one, and perhaps settle for less income. In the past you might have determined your own personal worth by the size of your paycheck. Is this one of your money fantasies? Does it assist you in any way in accomplishing your goal of freedom? This alignment process may actually provide you with an opportunity to relinquish a money fantasy that has been holding you hostage.

Another choice might be to decide to stick with the job, but give it an end point, reduce your spending and save your excess cash flow for when you leave

> *"This alignment process may actually provide you with an opportunity to relinquish a money fantasy that has been holding you hostage."*

that position. In other words, accumulate enough assets so that you can replace your return on labor cash flow with a return on assets cash flow. A third and similar option is to reduce your spending, saving the excess, so that when you choose to leave your job you have a financial cushion to use while you search for something that really does meet your needs. Using your imagination and creativity, you will find the choices are really endless.

The only choice that has no future is continuing to do what you have done in the past. If your present choices are not accomplishing your goal, namely, *freedom*, the only option is change. And since this is your life, rather than letting change happen to you, choose powerfully the changes that create the life you really want.

> *Budgeting is choosing consciously what you will spend and where.*

Next review your cash outflows in terms of your wants versus your needs. Are your wants and needs aligned with your goal? Do you see any needs that tend to excess? Do they have a significant component of want built in? If so, are these wants consistent with your goals and your prioritized strategies? If anything is out of alignment, simply choose differently.

Structure, in the form of a budget, can be helpful in making these changes. First, look to see if your existing definition of the word *budget* is about restriction, having less and limiting choices. If so, set your intention to let go of this self-defeating concept of budgeting before you begin. Remember, budgeting is choosing consciously what you will spend and where.

Budgets can also serve to liberate you in terms of fun spending. Once you are clear about how much you need to save for retirement, college, big-ticket items, etc., you are then free to enjoy the rest. Worry sets in when you aren't clear about how you are going to fund the necessities of life. Taking care of those necessities gives you freedom.

Prepare your budget with your future in mind. With the clarity you have about your priorities, go back and look at the way you are spending money. If your outflows are inconsistent with your goals, make a new choice.

Once you have a budget that is consistent with your goals and strategies, enter it into your checkbook management software. Track your spending against your budget, and review it at least monthly. If you are overspending in one area, choose another area to spend less in, or find a way to increase your cash flow.

Or, if this is too much detail for you, divide each paycheck into four categories:

1. The amount needed for savings such as retirement, big-ticket items, emergency cushion, and college.

2. The amount needed for larger non-recurring bills like insurance, real estate taxes, annual dues, fees and holidays.

3. The amount needed for your regular obligations, house payment, car payment, gas, etc.

4. The amount left over for your wants.

Prosperity Fable

Joe was seriously overextended in credit card debt. He was a teacher nearing retirement. He had a substantial pension available to him through teaching, but he needed to work the next five years to access it. He loved music and if he truly followed his passion, his work would be performing. After exploring his options with a money coach, Joe decided to continue teaching for another five years, and begin looking for opportunities to perform for small parties, gatherings and events. He committed to use the income from his music to clear up his credit card debt. He set his pricing and began telling people of his availability. Within two weeks he had his first event! In addition to making extra money, and getting himself out of credit card debt, he was living one of his dreams, to perform.

Set aside monies for your needs in categories one and two out of each paycheck. For example, if your car insurance is $600 every six months and you are paid weekly, you need to save $23 a week ($600 divided by 26 weeks) out of each check to have enough to cover your insurance premium when it comes due. Compute the weekly savings requirement for all the items in groups one and two. Write checks or use automatic withdrawals to fund your savings needs first. What is left is available for your wants and recurring bills.

Once you have aligned your cash flow with your goals and strategies, you may find that you are complete. That is, your present cash flow fully supports your goals and strategies.

For many, more is needed. Often no matter how you try, there is just not enough cash flow to meet your requirements. In this case, the only option is to increase your cash flow. Since you know that cash flow comes from four sources — return on labor, return on assets, return on a combination of assets and labor, and gifts — let's investigate the options with each one.

What are your options to increase return on labor? If you work for someone else:

- Get a second job

- Turn a hobby into income

- Get another, better-paying, full-time job

- Start your own business

In addition to these choices, once you put your thinking cap on, you will arrive at even more options. Remember to explore your opportunities carefully. Test your ideas. Find a way to try out your thoughts before you plunge. Think of it as putting your big toe in the bath water to check out the temperature before you get in. Don't make wholesale changes in your life until you are ready.

If you are self-employed, an array of choices are available. Begin by taking some time to look at your business as if it were not yours. Evaluate it as if you were considering buying it. Think strategically.

First make a list of what you have accomplished in your business. Change always has a more positive bend when you begin by affirming and appreciating your past.

Prosperity Insight

If you choose to start your own business be realistic. Most new businesses are not immediately profitable. Of course this depends on a host of issues. The best businesses are those where you do your homework. You know yourself and your gifts. You have researched the business marketplace. You are clear about your strategy and how it adds value, and you've given yourself the training you need to fulfill your roles in the business. In other words, like the scouts, be prepared!

> *Change always has a more positive bend when you begin by affirming and appreciating your past.*

Next, ask yourself these questions about your business:

- How can you make your business more profitable?
    - Should you hire a financial coach or consultant?
- Is your business saleable?
    - If so, how much is it worth and how much would you net after taxes?
    - What amount of return on assets would that produce?
- Is your business expandable?
- In what directions is the marketplace moving?
    - Is your business moving with it?
- What is holding your business back?
    - Is it a buggy whip business in the days of the automobile?
- What is your role in the business?
    - Are you replaceable?
    - Does being irreplaceable work for you?
- What makes your business unique?
    - What are your core differences?
- What are the key indicators of profitability in your business?
    - Do you have a monitoring system to track them?

- In each area of spending, are you getting a return on investment?

- What is working? What is not working? What is missing that would make it work?

To have a great business, you have to be clear about what your business contributes to the world, what is the marketplace for that contribution, and how to best serve that marketplace. Then you have to set up systems to market, manage and deliver that contribution, whether it is goods or services. You need systems to measure your performance to know when you are on target. And you will need to continually reassess your strategic position to determine if it still makes sense.

There are thousands of resources for improving the profitability of your business. Check out the business section of your local library or bookstore. Notice what ideas speak to you. Ask business colleagues you admire about how they grew their businesses.

Consider your options for increasing your return on labor carefully, and then choose what is right for you. Celebrate and appreciate your successes.

Prosperity Insight

It is challenging to look objectively at your own business. Using the analogy of a forest, if you spend your days working in your business, you could say you spend your days in the forest. Being in the forest, your perspective is from within. To really analyze your business strategically and move it in a more prosperous direction requires that you are able to see the entire forest. As long as you are in the forest, that is impossible. So you must change your perspective before you can really look at your business strategically. Often the best way to access this perspective is via a coach or consultant. Bringing a person in who already has an outside perspective can be invaluable in assisting you in shifting your own view. You can find a Certified Public Accountant, CPA, who specializes in consulting at **http://www.ranone.com.**

At this point let's look at how to increase your return on asset income stream.

There are four basic ways to create or increase your return on assets cash flow. These strategies may be used separately or in tandem.

Personal Insight

I coach people daily to grow and prosper in their businesses. But when it comes to my own business, I use a coach. Without a coach I fall into one of several convenient traps. One is that I will make emotional decisions. My Enneagram type is in the emotional center, so it is natural for me to access this way of being. However it does not always serve my best interest. To take care of myself, I set up coaching arrangements where I have access to my coach when I get the urge to make dramatic, rash decisions. I call and tell my coach what I am thinking rather than confusing my team and driving them crazy! We all have strengths and weaknesses. One of the best gifts you can give yourself and those around you is to know your own.

The first is to take a portion of your return on labor cash flow and invest it wisely in assets. This is the traditional way most people save for retirement or financial independence. Over time enough assets are accumulated to produce sufficient cash flow to fund your lifestyle.

The second way is to convert some of your lifestyle assets to investment assets. Review your financial position. Do you own lifestyle assets that you underutilize or perhaps are less attached to than when you purchased them?

For example, maybe you have a vacation home but use it very little. Consider selling it or renting it out. Look at your goals and strategies. Is owning a rarely used vacation home a fit with your goals? Or would you facilitate reaching your goals by converting the vacation home to an asset that produces cash flow?

Another illustration is collectibles. Do you own a gun or coin collection? Do you collect antiques? Does owning these items fit with your goals and strategies? Or would you be closer to *The Intersection of Joy and Money* if you sold them and converted the cash to investment assets?

As an added bonus, you may find that you have a rider on your homeowners insurance to cover your collectibles. Converting them to investment assets may reduce your need for insurance and free up additional cash flow.

Yet another example is to downsize your home and invest the savings. If you are an empty nester, look to see if moving into a smaller, less expensive home fits your goals.

The third and more complex way is to see if something you have created can be turned into an investment asset.

We have already discussed the idea that a closely held business and real estate can be a combination return on assets and return on labor. If your labor is required in the business or real estate, it is a hybrid. One way to increase your return on assets is to systematize your business processes so that your labor is not required. Then you have created a return on asset out of an investment of your labor.

Here is a simple example. Compare these two consulting firms. One is a one-person firm where the owner sells his services by the hour, day or project. This owner manages the work, sells the work and does the work. The second is a firm with three employees. This company has a consulting process, which is documented with each phase clearly defined. The owner's responsibilities are articulated, as are those of the two key employees. Each person is cross-trained in the jobs of the other. The owner could easily choose to hire a CEO to replace herself. She could move to an overview position of a board member, where the new CEO is accountable to her, allowing her to focus her efforts elsewhere. If she chose to do so, she may have less total return from the business due to the additional employee cost, but she would have virtually all her time to focus on other activities.

In the example, the first owner has a business, but the return from the business is return on labor. He cannot walk away from the business, and it has no value without him. The second owner has a company that is positioned to move into a return-on-assets model. The business is run via systems and processes, and the owner is replaceable. Both have the opportunity to take their business and convert it to a return-on-assets model, but the second owner is much closer to this possibility.

The entire rise of dot-com companies exemplifies taking an idea, investing labor and converting the idea to a return on assets. Unfortunately, at least in the short term, the financial markets were a little over-zealous with the ideas, over-investing in unproven models. This does not mean many of these ideas will not work, or that they ultimately might not be incredibly successful. What you have seen with this boom and bust is that the fundamental premise of business — that a business must make a profit to be successful — is unchanged.

Because there is no limit to ideas, there is no limit to the ways you can create investment asset cash flow from a return on labor investment. Generally some assets, or *capital* as it is usually referred to in business, is required. So whatever your idea, generally you have to invest some of your own capital before others are willing to take a risk as well. Your first step, then, is to find and save some excess cash flow.

Think of some of the giant companies of the world, such as IBM, Proctor and Gamble, Microsoft, General Electric. They all started with someone's great idea. Often this idea was not original, but rather brought a product or service to market in a unique way, or slightly altered the way things were previously done. The bottom line is that to have a viable business you must add value. Those who find creative ways to do this are ultimately successful.

Remember the fifth truth about money: *Money is energy and has value because we all agree that it does.* This is the principle upon which these great ideas became successful businesses. They added value beyond what was previously in existence, and people were willing to pay for that.

The fourth way to increase the return on asset income is to find underutilized investment assets and increase their return. An example is the simplest way to explore this idea. Let's look at a prosperity fable.

> *Because there is no limit to ideas, there is no limit to the ways you can create investment asset cash flow from a return on labor investment.*

Prosperity Fable

Jane and John opened a service business in 1970 in an area of quick population growth. Thirty years later they find themselves with a prime piece of real estate, surrounded by fast food and gas stations. The fair market value of their property is $750,000, which they determined by reviewing real estate records of sales occurring near them. They could rent sufficient space to operate their business for $3000 a month, or $36,000 a year. If they sold the real estate and simply paid the capital gains tax, their CPA tells them they would net $620,000 from the transaction. In their opinion, a comfortable rate of return on this money if invested in a diversified portfolio is 8%, which is $49,600. They could then relocate their business and produce an additional $13,600 ($49,600 less $36,000) a year cash flow.

This idea, converting underutilized investment assets into an increase in cash flow is a more complex idea. Unless you have a substantial finance background yourself, these ideas may be best suited for review by your financial planner.

Let's look again at the components of your money life:

- Money habits of mind
- Goals and strategies
- Current cash flow
- Future cash flow
- Planning for big-ticket items
- Current net worth
- Liquidity
- Risk management
- Financial independence

- Estate planning

- Income tax planning

- College funding

- Investment planning and management

- Aligning work with your essence
  and passion

You can see that everything is impacted by your cash flow. Whatever your dreams, they only materialize with cash flow. While many financial planners and much financial planning theory revolves around asset accumulation, ultimately the assets must produce cash flow or the plan fails. That is why it is critical that before you engage a financial planner, you know what cash flow you require to make your life work, now and in the future. Ultimately all planning is about bringing this into reality.

> *Everything is impacted by your cash flow.*

As you continue to bring alignment of your goals and strategies with your cash flow, you also begin to address each area of your money life. For example, your income taxes directly impact your available cash flow. If you choose to use life insurance in your estate planning, that too affects your cash flow. If you choose to redesign your business to be more of an expression of who you really are, that can significantly impact your cash flow.

To bring the third truth of money, *That each piece of your money life gives you the whole*, into present reality, let's revisit each area.

As you review each area, go as in depth with your own study as it is your nature. Internet references are provided, and there are local classes, libraries and bookstores, all pouring over with financial planning technical material. However, you may not be a detail person. If so, allow yourself the opportunity to simply read through the material on each area, and use it as background to help you choose a financial planner. Discern what is right for you.

Money habits of mind

> *Just remember your life is a work in progress; therefore, so is your life with money.*

You tackled this area in Chapter Six. Just remember your life is a work in progress; therefore so is your life with money. You have thousands of money messages, some of which are helpful and others not. While the exercises are supportive in uncovering your habits of mind around money, more will unfold as you move through life. There may be much more subtle yet powerful messages that you have yet to access. All there is to do is notice the results you are getting. If they are not what you intended consciously, look again at your money history.

Goals and strategies

The information and work you did in Chapter Eight distinguished goals and strategies and provided clarity about your priorities. If you choose to use an advisor, this is the most important information you have to convey to him or her.

You may also choose to use an advisor to help you clarify your goals and strategies, and to uncover your money habits of mind. If is often easier for someone outside yourself to see what is limiting you. There

Prosperity Fable

A psychology professor was teaching the process of conditioned reflex as first documented by Pavlov (**http://www.pbs.org**) in his experiments with dogs. Pavlov would ring a bell every time he fed his dogs. After some time, he just rang the bell, no longer presenting food. The dogs salivated just as if food were present. The professor's class decided to try out this conditioning theory on their teacher. They had noticed that he paced to and fro when he lectured. The class decided that when he walked to their right they would non-verbally attend to his lecture, by taking notes and using eye contact. When he walked to the left they would stop attending by looking away, and ceasing taking notes. No verbal words were spoken by the students. Within the fifty-minute class period, the professor was standing on the right, not moving to and fro as he had in every class previous. Ask yourself, if a professor can be *taught* in fifty minutes where to stand in a classroom with all non-verbal training, imagine what you have learned over a lifetime of informal training.

are professional money coaches and life coaches. Some financial planners will help you in this area as well.

Current cash flow

The work in Chapter Seven elucidated your current cash flow. Earlier in this chapter you looked at a variety of ways to improve your cash flow. An advisor can help you look at your cash flow objectively and assist you with choosing the methods of improving cash flow that are right for you. Just remember, you need to do the basic work in Chapter Seven prior to seeing your planner. If you cannot get through the materials yourself, get as far as you can on your own and take what you accomplish to your planner.

Future cash flow

Your current cash flow along with your goals and strategies should give you a picture of your future cash flow. It is your future cash flow that your retirement savings is intended to fund, so knowing this is critical to properly planning for happy years after work. Many planners suggest that you use a percentage of your current spending as your retirement spending. Do not be caught in this trap. You will have more leisure in your retirement, and while your children will be grown, you may very well have grandchildren you will enjoy spoiling.

Instead of a percentage, just take each category of spending, and ask, *Will I spend less in this area in retirement?* Also ask, *Will I spend more?* You will be surprised at just how little less you intend to spend.

Use this information to generate your savings plan. Draw on the Internet as a resource for financial calculators, or take this information to the planner you hire.

Planning for big-ticket items

Your goals and strategies should tell you clearly what your needs and wants are in this area. Use a separate savings account for the money you are saving for large expenditures. Do not commingle these funds with other monies.

Current net worth

Chapter Seven gave you a clear picture of your current net worth or financial position. Your investment assets are a piece of the puzzle for your retirement savings. Give this information to your planner, or plug it into an Internet financial calculator.

Liquidity

As part of your financial plan, you need a liquidity plan. You need liquid monies available to you for emergency purposes, such as short-term disability or job loss. You may also tap your liquidity fund to live on temporarily while you start your own business or change jobs. Good planning is to have three to six months' spending in a savings account. If you spend $3000 a month, your liquidity fund should be $9000 to $18,000. Keep these funds in a savings or money market account.

The goal for these monies is to give you security in bad times; their return is insignificant. If you do not have an emergency fund, make this a top priority on your list of strategies.

Personal Insight

One of the most positive role models I had in my formative years around money was an aunt on my mother's side. She lived on her own and was one of the few women I knew who took care of herself financially. I adored her. She would visit often, and while at our home, would give me her *money rules of life.* She had many great ones. One of the best was always save a little extra for those big-ticket items along the way, a new car, a new roof, etc. She followed her own advice and continues to be a financial role model for me.

Risk management

You may think of risk management as insurance, but it includes other aspects such as doing what is necessary in your life to avoid inappropriate risk, and taking appropriate risk.

If you make your living as a surgeon, doing activities that have a great danger of damaging your hands may be more risk than you can afford. If you are the only breadwinner in your family and your children are young, the risk of taking up mountain climbing may be too great! So what is appropriate for you depends on your individual circumstances.

Automobile insurance is a way to illustrate. The deductible is the amount of risk you can afford to take. If it is challenging for you to pay for a $100 unexpected loss, you may require a like deductible. If you have funded your liquidity plan, and/or have significant disposable income, a $500 unanticipated loss may be of no consequence. When your children begin driving, you may decide to buy them an inexpensive car and take no collision coverage on it at all. So the risk that you can afford to take varies with your own personal situation.

When you take appropriate risk, such as a higher deductible, you lower the cash outflow (premium) required for insurance, because you are assuming a higher risk and the insurance company is assuming a lower risk.

Insurance, which is spreading the risks among many, is a part of your overall risk management plan, as is your assessment of how much risk you can accept and afford.

Let's look at the areas where you need to manage risk:

Health insurance

Your financial plan must provide adequate health insurance. The most affordable health insurance is generally employer-provided. Consider this first, as you will find group coverage substantially less than individual coverage. While you will pay less with a group plan, you will often have fewer choices, so there is a trade off.

If you are self-employed, look into a high deductible plan with a medical savings account. Unfortunately these are not available in every state, but if they are offered where you live, check them out.

Find out more at
http://www.moneycentral.com

Life insurance

Life insurance is one of the most oversold insurance products in existence. It is often sold out of fear, with little relationship to personal goals.

There are really just three reasons to purchase life insurance. One is to provide an asset base, which can be used to replace your income stream for a

Prosperity Insight

As a society we have moved significantly to HMO type coverage, which goes against the fundamental principles of risk management discussed above. Risk management is accepting affordable risk, and most can afford more than a ten, twenty or thirty dollar co-pay. Money is energy, and in the HMO environment, being sick has little money or energetic consequences. At a physical level doing what is needed for your wellness is self-responsible. HMOs are a model of irresponsibility in that their low co-pay model makes frequent care visits affordable and sustainable, giving little or no incentive for wellness behavior. As a society, if we are to solve our health insurance crisis, it requires we remember the purpose of insurance: to cover catastrophic costs, not to pay for everyday living expenses.

dependent spouse or minor children. If others are depending on you, life insurance is a must. Generally term insurance will do, which is cheaper than universal or whole life. Term is perfect for a short-term need. As you age, you are accumulating assets for your financial independence, which in turn produce increasing cash inflow. Therefore, your need for this type of life insurance diminishes naturally.

You can determine your need for income stream replacement insurance at **http://www.quicken.com**. At the site, go to *insurance quotes, life*. Review the site **http://www.intelliquote.com** to understand more about term insurance. The site **http://www.accuquote.com** gives a comprehensive review of life insurance terms.

The second need for life insurance is to provide liquidity to a non-liquid estate. If your estate is primarily composed of assets not readily marketable, such as a closely held business or real estate, your heirs may find themselves with significant estate tax at your death, but little cash to pay it. Remember the Fifth Money Truth — *money has value because we all agree*. If your heirs must sell assets quickly to generate cash to pay the estate tax, they will be at a significant disadvantage in their quest for a fair price, as they will be under pressure to sell. If your estate requires this type of insurance, it is best acquired through using an irrevocable life insurance trust.

Find out more about irrevocable life insurance trusts and estate taxes at **http://www.nafep.com**.

Review http://www.nafep.com for general financial planning information.

The third reason to purchase life insurance is to replace the erosion of your estate from estate taxes at your death. Let's say you have an estate of $3 million, and your estate taxes will be $600,000, leaving your heirs $2.4 million. If one of your strategies is to leave your heirs as much as possible, you can purchase replacement life insurance of $600,000. This brings the assets available to your heirs to $3 million. If this is part of your plan, again use an irrevocable life insurance trust.

To find out more about the different types of insurance, go to http://www.accuquote.com.

Prosperity Insight

Before you commit to a large permanent insurance contract, have your needs reviewed by a planner who does not sell insurance. Most insurance is sold on a commission basis; accordingly the agent is compensated more for a larger policy. Be sure you have someone acting in your best interest in an unbiased manner before you purchase.

Disability insurance

Disability is your biggest risk. Between the ages of twenty-five and fifty-five you are twice as likely to be disabled for more than ninety days than you are to die. Yet while most people have life insurance, few carry disability insurance. Realize as well that disability is much more of a burden on your family. If you are disabled, not only will you not be able to work, you will require care of some type. For these reasons, disability coverage is a must unless you are financially independent.

Find out more about disability insurance at http://www.life-line.org.

Property and casualty insurance

If you own property you cannot afford to replace in the event of a disaster, you need property and casualty insurance. Typically this is homeowners coverage, renters insurance, and automobile coverage.

Check out http://www.insure.com for a comprehensive insurance information resource.

Long-term care insurance

According to the Health Insurance Association of America you face a seventy percent chance of needing nursing home care if you are over sixty-five. You would probably prefer a private nurse to facility care. All this costs money.

If you want to maintain your dignity and your estate, consider long-term care insurance. You probably do not need to consider this coverage until you are in your early fifties, at which time you should investigate it seriously.

Review http://www.consumerlawpage.com or http://www.longtermcareinsurance.com for more information on long-term care.

Umbrella liability

Unfortunately, you and I live in a society where people settle their disputes in court rather than in conversations. This type of policy picks up where your homeowners and automobile coverage ends. It is very affordable.

If you have significant assets and want to protect them, consider an umbrella policy. Contact the agent for your property and casualty insurance for this coverage.

Financial independence

Retirement is a wonderful objective, but perhaps more fulfilling is the concept of financial independence, where you have sufficient assets that you no longer need to work, but can if you so choose. Whether your work is so gratifying that you would engage in it regardless of the financial results, or you work only as a means to an end, having a choice about whether to go to work or not is the ultimate freedom.

The following web sites can help you calculate what you need to save for retirement:

http://www.kiplinger.com
http://www.usnews.com
http://www.quicken.com.

To gather information on the impact of social security benefits on your retirement go to http://www.ssa.gov.

" Having a choice about whether to go to work or not is the ultimate freedom. "

Estate planning

Estate planning is letting others know how you want things handled at your death and planning in advance how much of your estate will be given to the federal and state governments.

The first challenge is to decide what you want to happen in the event of your death. How do you want your assets distributed? Who do you want to take care of things? What are your desires in terms of burial? The more complex your financial situation is during your life, the more complex your estate planning issues.

These questions are documented using the legal tools of a will, trust, power of attorney, and letter of instruction. You may need one or all of these documents. At the very least you need a simple will clearly delineating your wishes. Once prepared, review these documents every three to seven years. If your family status changes in any way, change your documents accordingly.

This area is complex. The best estate plans are those done in consultation with a financial planner and an attorney focusing in this area. Review the jargon and general area of estate planning at:
http://www.estateplanninglinks.com
http://www.nafep.com.

Both the federal and most state governments impose estate tax. There are many strategies for avoiding or reducing estate taxes. If you do nothing, and your estate is large enough, the government will take a portion of the assets you accumulated over your lifetime for the U.S. Treasury. If that fits your goals and strategies, you need not do anything about your estate tax.

Find the current federal estate tax rates at
http://www.estateplanninglinks.com.

This site also gives you a variety of other sites, which have information on a variety of estate planning topics.

If you do not want to support the federal treasury with your assets, review the estate planning ideas at http://www.savewealth.com. In addition the sites listed above that have general estate planning information also have tax reduction strategies.

Income tax planning

Do not confuse having your income tax return professionally prepared — that is, income tax preparation — with income tax planning. They are fundamentally two different services. When you hire someone to prepare your returns, what you get is assistance with completing the forms. They may offer suggestions for deductions, or record keeping, but it is all after the fact.

Income tax planning is strategically looking ahead at your income tax picture for the purpose of paying the least tax legally. Quality tax planning includes advice on documenting deductions, appropriate record keeping, strategies to defer tax, and strategies to eliminate tax. In other words, a comprehensive review of your situation.

When you consult your advisor, be clear whether you are engaging in one or both of these areas. If you have a simple return, and you are comfortable with your tax knowledge, consider preparing your return using one of the on-line or home tax packages.

While doing your own research is helpful, get professional expertise for tax planning. Income tax law is complex and confusing. Income tax is also your largest single expense. What better way to free up additional cash flow than to reduce taxes? Consider your tax planning service an investment in your current cash flow, and ultimately in your enhanced financial position.

College funding

Children often turn out wonderfully no matter what their parents choose.

There are as many ways to go about college funding as there are colleges. What is right for you is a personal decision. Perhaps you want to provide fully paid tuition, room and board through graduate school. Perhaps you want to assist your children with tuition, while they live at home. Perhaps you will pay in-state tuition, but if your children want to go out of state, or to a private college, they will pay the difference. There is no right or wrong. More importantly, children often turn out wonderfully no matter what their parents choose.

After you have answered the question of what level of support you want to provide then review your funding options. You could create a savings plan. You can use a Section 529 plan which is a type of educational plan that allows tax-deferred growth of your assets. There are educational IRAs, prepaid tuition plans, and there are UTMA (Uniform Transfer to Minors Act) or UGMA (Uniform Gift to Minors Act) accounts. In addition there are significant income tax incentives if you qualify. Review the options at:
http://www.collegeplanning.org
http://www.kiplinger.com
http://www.usnews.com.

Lastly, if you have insufficient cash flow to fund both retirement and college savings needs, fund your retirement. The compounding effect of money over time (remember the Rule of Seventy-two in Chapter Three?) will make quite a difference in your retirement planning. If you begin work at age twenty-two, and retire at sixty-two, you have forty years for your money to compound. If you have a child, and begin saving immediately, you have no more than eighteen years to save for college. This means that compounding helps, but not to the extent it does with retirement funding.

If your cash flow limitations require that you choose to fund only retirement, then pay for college out of your cash flow when your child is in school. You can do this partially by not funding your retirement during this period. You will come out better in the long run, because the money you have accumulated for retirement will still be compounding even when you are not adding it each year.

If in the long run you cannot save for college, or pay for it out of your current cash flow, there are also student loans, scholarships and grants. In today's environment, anyone who really wants a college education can get one.

Investment planning and management

You will notice that in the flow of components investment planning and management is near the end. Most people have a tendency to begin here. And many financial advisors focus only on this area. But investments are just like any other piece of your

> *Realize there is no such thing as a perfect company with an immaculate social record. We live in a world of ambiguity and change.*

money life — they are just one piece. To address investment planning and management without addressing your goals, strategies, cash flow, etc, is to begin a journey across the ocean without a destination or a compass. In order for you to accomplish what you want in life, the focus has to be on you. Said another way, it is easy to get where you are going if you have no destination.

Do not be swayed by financial planners who want to put you in a box and have an investment plan for you based on your age. You are unique, you are not a model. What is appropriate is for you to discern with guidance from your resources. For the very best results from your financial plan, address all the areas of your money life before you address investment management. At the very least, be clear on your goals and strategies, prepare your investment plan, and subsequently reassess your investments as you complete the remainder of your plan.

The web is filled with sites on investment planning and management. Here are a few:
http://www.usnews.com
http://www.moneycentral.com
http://www.bloomberg.com
http://www.fool.com
http://www.thestreet.com.

The Enron, Tyco and MCI events, just to name a few, have left a credibility gap. Historically, audited financial statements were relied upon as an accurate picture of a company's past. These statements, along with management growth forecasts, formed the basis upon which analysts predicted future stock prices.

Virtually all analysis focused solely on the company's financial past and future.

For the last twenty years, a new way of investing has emerged, Socially Responsible Investing (SRI). SRI investing does not look just at historical and future profits; it also examines the corporate value system. Are employees treated with disrespect? Does the company destroy or damage the environment? Do company products cause illness, disease and death? Does the company practice sustainability? Does the company produce products that are harmful to animals or humans? SRI investing looks for profitability and growth, along with a value system that protects the future of our planet, respects the dignity of people and has integrity.

I believe that the only investments that have long-term merit are in the Socially Responsible area. For we must foster a healthy planet, practice dignity relative to the human spirit and have integrity to have a future. At the same time realize there is no such thing as a perfect company with an immaculate social record. We live in a world of ambiguity and change. SRI investing is about finding companies that are moving in a positive, progressive manner toward a better planet.

Another beauty in the SRI world is that you decide what is responsible. There are many ways to go about this quest of alignment. You may choose to avoid certain industries completely. You may search primarily for companies focused on enhancing human dignity. You decide what *social responsibility* means to you.

We know that people alter when given a financial incentive. SRI investing is like voting with your money. You make a private, personal choice, which has the potential to transform business to a future model of ethics and sustainability. What is required is the intention to make a difference and a little more homework. When you select your investments, choose from a place consistent with your personal values, and invest in companies with growth prospects and integrity-based management. To invest any other way is just a statement of fear.

> *SRI investing is like voting with your money.*

If you would like more information on this area, here are some web sites:
http://www.goodmoney.com
http://www.greenmoneyjournal.com
http://www.srinvest.net

Along with investing with your values, practice the principle of diversification. Have your investments in a variety of assets: small-cap stocks, mid-cap stocks, and large-cap stocks; government bonds; short-term bonds, intermediate-term bonds and long-term bonds; real estate; and commodities. And don't forget yourself and your closely held business. Money has value because we all agree. What the collective society treasures at any one point in time is not something you can control. Plan your life so that it works regardless of the whims of *groupthink*.

Aligning work with your essence and passion

Prosperity includes having the financial resources to claim your dreams. For most people, work is what provides these resources.

Truth Five is that *money is energy*. When you expend personal energy in work, you are rewarded in a unit we call *money*. To live your life at *The Intersection of Joy and Money* requires that the personal energy you expend to get money be a joyous process. Simply said, your work must be joyful.

The most joy-filled place to work is at *The Intersection of your Essence and Passion*. Your essence is a gift or gifts you were born with. You did not learn these talents in school — you have always had them. They are innate. When you are in your essence work is effortless, therefore it is not draining. You end your work day with as much or more energy than when you began. Your passion is what puts fire in your belly. What gives you energy? When you lose track of space and time, what are you doing? What do you want to contribute to the world? What story of your work life have you repeated because you felt so good about your success?

Personal Insight

To support myself in transitioning from business owner to fully expressed entrepreneur, I engaged in a personal-growth program designed to master risk. The six-month course, called Cliff Jumping, offered weekly coaching sessions and monthly classroom sessions with other participants. While there are many avenues to personal growth, I've found that the most profound require individual accountability. In Cliff Jumping, I was required to state my goal, which was to convert my role in my business to one where I was engaged in my essence and passion. I was held accountable for my progress through the weekly coaching sessions and monthly peer meetings. Taking on change — risk — was possible for me because I was not doing it alone.

> *Your essence is a gift or gifts you were born with…*
>
> *Your passion is what puts fire in your belly.*

This is an inner search. It requires intimate knowledge of the most important person in your life — you. And the rewards for living a life that serves and contributes, while fulfilling you at a very personal level, are infinite. It is worth the journey to discover this place inside yourself.

You have now looked at each area of your money life. You have a clear idea of what you want to accomplish. Your goals and strategies are articulated and documented. You understand your cash flow and financial position. You have reviewed all the areas of your financial life. At this point you either are ready for professional guidance or you feel confident using the Internet, books or other resources to work through your plan on your own.

Congratulations! ∎

Summary

✔ Clarity about your goals and strategies provides a foundation to review each piece of your money life.

✔ Use the power of choice to align your actions in each area of your money life with your goals.

Chapter

10

Path Four:
Congruent
Action:
Using Advisors

*If your experiences would benefit
anybody, give them to someone.*

— Florence Nightingale

*F*or most, the world of money is too complex to manage without professional advice. Because money is a sensitive subject, you may tend to avoid seeking advice, or just plain be confused about how and who to hire.

Remember, you aren't ready for any kind of specialized advice until you have built your foundation, meaning you have worked through your money fantasies, and have an understanding of your cash flow and financial position. If you seek specialized advice prior to forming your foundation, you may be abdicating rather than assuming responsibility for your money life. Your advisor or advisors aren't in the picture to take care of you; that is your job. Hiring an advisor is a powerful way to take responsibility for yourself, but only after your foundation is built.

Here are some general guidelines for hiring any advisor.

Rule One

Know both how and how much your advisor is paid. Do not hire anyone with whom you are unwilling to discuss compensation. Also do not hire anyone unwilling to tell you how he or she gets paid, and the amount. As human beings we respond to our reward systems. Until you know your advisor's reward system (how she gets paid) do not proceed.

> *Determine if your value system is congruent with your advisor.*

Rule Two

Gather information until you are comfortable. Don't act on blind faith. You may be tempted to hire a friend of a friend, or someone with whom you socialize, and that can be great, as long as you are willing to ask the hard questions. *What are your credentials? How long have you been in business? What kind of clients do you have? What is your process? How are you compensated?* Unless you are willing to ask these questions do not proceed.

Rule Three

Find out your advisor's reputation in the community. Ask around and find out how this person is seen in the community. References may be helpful. If an advisor cannot give you at least one or two names of clients who are happy with her services, you probably don't want to use her.

Rule Four

Determine if your value system is congruent with your advisor. Ask questions about how your advisor makes decisions. Find out if he or she has a socially responsible screening process. Ask how you can apply screens to the process. Inquire about the advisor's views on diversification. Understand how your advisor will communicate with you, how often and in what form.

Rule Five

Follow your intuition. Everyone has intuition. You know when something is a *yes* for you.

Today's environment is confusing. There is so much technical information. To make matters worse, there are specialists in everything, and it seems everybody has initials. What do all these initials mean?

A comprehensive list of financial planning designations can be found at http://www.financial-designations.8m.com and http://www.cfp-board.org.

Regardless of credentials, there are three ways planners can get paid: commission only, fee and commission, and fee only.

Commission-only planners get paid by selling products ranging from insurance and annuities to mutual funds and stocks. These planners may help you with a financial plan, but it is usually a generic, canned, computer-generated plan and with little personalized consultation. They offer advice on plan execution, which is generally focused on product sales.

Fee and commission planners are also called fee-based planners and commonly charge a flat or hourly fee for a financial plan. They also sell products of the same type as commission-only planners. Often their plans are relatively inexpensive, as most of their income is from commissions. However, as with commission-based planners, their plans are fairly generic and canned.

Fee-only planners may state their fees in a variety of ways. Fees may be on a per-hour basis, such as $125 or $200 an hour, or a per-job basis, such as $5000 for a comprehensive financial plan. In addition or in lieu of flat fee or hourly rates, they may also charge quarterly or annual retainers, which are either flat fees or based on your assets. Their plans are typically tailored to your individual circumstance.

> *While the cost of a fee-only planner may seem high when you first consider this option, remember it is human to react to your reward system.*

While the cost of a fee-only planner may seem high when you first consider this option, remember it is human to react to your reward system. A financial plan is a long-term investment. You want to work with someone you can trust, and with whom you have an open and responsive relationship. If you hire someone who gets paid primarily from selling you a product, that is, a commission-only or fee and commission planner, how will you ever be sure you got the best advice for your personal situation?

Begin by identifying advisors to select from. Ask your friends and colleagues for references, search the web, and look in the local phone directory. Gather at least two, preferably three names.

Call each and ask about their client selection process. If their client criteria and your circumstances are a match, ask about an initial consultation. Most advisors will not charge for a first appointment to talk with you about their services. They may also offer a way to introduce you to their services at a low cost, or a service guarantee.

Consider the characteristics you want in your planner, such as responsibility, honesty, communication, competence, commitment to your success. The best planners act as educators and are great listeners. Make a list before you go to your initial appointment. This way you are focused on what is important to you.

If your advisor gives investment advice, he or she will have a form ADV (Advisor Disclosure Voucher). This form is filed annually with the SEC and/or the applicable state regulatory body. The ADV contains a wealth of information including a list of credentials and the details on how the planner charges.

When hiring an advisor, you can hire one advisor to take care of your entire financial plan, or you can hire different professionals to take care of their own particular area. Obviously hiring one advisor is the easy and convenient way. Consider if you have concerns in many areas of your money life, or just a few. If there are just a few, looking for an advisor who specializes narrowly in that area may be best for you.

After you have completed your interviews and checked backgrounds and references, choose the candidate with whom you had the best rapport. Make an appointment and get started. Take your goals, strategies, cash flow and financial position with you to the meeting. If you were unable to complete any of this on your own, that is where you will need to begin. Always build a solid foundation before you go any further. ■

The best planners act as educators and are great listeners.

Summary

✔ Hiring an advisor is a powerful way to take responsibility for yourself.

✔ Human beings respond to reward systems. Understand exactly how your advisor gets paid.

✔ Know your values and ask your advisor about hers.

✔ Follow your intuition.

Path Five:
Reassessment

*We aren't what we ought to be.
We aren't what we're going to
be. We aren't what we want to
be. But, thank God, we aren't
where we were.*

— Anonymous

G rowth is never done or complete. You are always evolving. And so must your money life.

Being at *The Intersection of Joy and Money* requires that you look again. You may change, therefore reassessment is necessary. Or you may find the path you set really isn't serving you. That is OK. Since you are creating your life by choice, it is as simple as choosing again.

You may find new opportunities. Things you never dreamed possible when you began your journey come into reality, and you see the possibility for the first time. This is a result of your growth and development. It may also be divine guidance. From whatever source this new awareness comes, welcome it and be open to trying it out.

Go back through your Goals and Strategies exercise, and see what is at the core of *you*. See if your new opportunities are a fit for that core. Choose appropriately.

Life is like a trip down a river for the first time. You can plan for the journey, but until you get to the bend in the stream you really don't know what is ahead. Your job is to stay true to your goals and navigate the new water, focusing on how you are best served. This way, the path around the obstacles will always appear.

> *You are always evolving. And so must your money life.*

My Own Path to Joy

As for the eight-year-old who stole from her best friend, I am now forty-seven. I live a life of prosperity. I spend my days doing work I absolutely

> *Once I got out of fear and accepted my power, life altered quickly.*

love. I have great friends and a wonderful loving family. I get pleasure from my client relationships. I have all the material things I desire. I am intellectually challenged. My piggy bank is now a diversified portfolio. Because I have invested in my own growth and development, I have more self-awareness and self-esteem than ever in my life. I have a strong spiritual community. I travel frequently. I engage in public speaking that makes a difference. And I have completed this book and my own journey to *The Intersection of Joy and Money*.

My life is my creation. To get to this place has taken me years and many leaps of faith. I had to heal past emotional wounds. Many times I wanted to turn back. To run away from the uprooted old pain which felt unending. But I stayed true to my goal, to fill my life with joy. And even when it seemed impossible that this was the path to joy, it was.

As I look back, I see the sacredness of my journey. Once I got out of fear and accepted my power, life altered quickly. It was my own resistance that complicated my transformation. Now when I find life confusing or joy absent, I choose again. Life is meant to be joyful. ■

12 Steps to Successful Achievement

1. In a notebook, dedicated to your goal-setting program, write all of your desires, no matter how large or how small.

2. Choose the 12 most important desires and write them on this card in order of importance to you. Be very specific.

3. Be open and receptive to change. Pray daily, "Father, what must I change about myself in order to achieve my goals?"

4. Determine the date by which you desire to achieve each goal.

5. Read your goals at least three times every morning and every evening.

6. Imagine yourself achieving each goal.

7. Accept your success now. Act as if you had already achieved.

8. Take positive action, in faith toward your goals; believe you receive.

9. Don't tell others. Keep your goals private, between you and God.

10. Cross off the goals as they are achieved and continue to add new ones.

11. Tithe 10% (at least) of all you receive to God's work where you receive your spiritual food.

12. Remember, God's highest law is Love.

—Edwene Gaines

Now go and seek your fortune, darling.

— Angela Carter

My Story

My Story

*O*ur culture teaches that body, mind and soul are separate. My belief is that they are all one. Through personal experience I have come to believe that true healing occurs at all levels. I am not talking about the kind of healing our culture engages in where you take a pill to repress the symptoms. I am speaking of the kind wholeness that occurs when you remove blocked energy, thereby allowing your body to renew itself naturally.

My first experience with this type of healing came as a result of a challenge with my left eye. I was driving back to my office one morning following an appointment. Suddenly the road was blurry. This lasted a few seconds and my normal perfect vision returned. In a minute or two it happened again. I was frantic! Fearing that I might wreck my car and hurt myself or someone else, I got back to my office as quickly as I could. I was relieved to be non-mobile and terrified of what had just happened. My vision continued to alter from clear to blurry. My imagination ran rampant — cancer, a brain tumor, some kind of degenerative disease that was taking away my eyesight — the horrible possibilities seemed endless.

I called my eye doctor in a panic and went to see him that afternoon. He ran every possible test, but found nothing. Trying to reassure me, he told me my eyes were healthy. He recommended I see a neurologist. I took his advice. Following the appointment with the neurologist, I had an MRI and consulted an ear, nose and throat specialist. I was tested, poked and prodded until I was weary. No change in my vision, still random moments of fuzziness followed by panic.

Sitting in church one day, I decided to close one eye when the blurred vision occurred. To my surprise, if I closed my left eye, I could see perfectly. I had stumbled across the truth that whatever was happening was only in my left eye. With this new information I returned to the neurologist. This time his diagnosis was a twitch in the muscles surrounding my left eye. I was relieved to know that my problem was as simple as a muscle twitch. He offered me a prescription. I asked how long and often I would take this medication. *Daily and forever,* he replied.

Taking a pill for the rest of my life was not for me. I thanked him and left. Having no idea what I was going to do next, I went home for some quiet time. Sitting in my favorite chair, I picked up a magazine and noticed an article on energy healers. With eagerness, I read it. It was worth a try. The question was, where would I find an energy healer?

Two days later I walked into a party, and after greeting a friend, asked, *Do you know an energy healer?* To my surprise her answer was, *Yes I do, and she is great!* I called the next morning for an appointment.

Nervously, I knocked on the door. A voice called, *it's open.* I let myself in. She smiled, gave me a hug, and escorted me to her simple workroom, where a table covered with crystals, a chair and a massage table greeted me. She requested that I lie down on the massage table and asked if I wanted a blanket. *Yes,* I replied. The blanket helped calm my jitters in this new and uncertain environment.

She told me that I could sleep or stay awake. That her work would proceed regardless of my state. She began by holding one of her crystals in her right hand and swirling it over my body. *I am feeling your energy,* she explained. I had not told her why I was there, but she immediately asked about my left eye. She explained that she could feel the energy block over my eye and asked me if I had sustained an injury of some sort. I explained that four years ago, I had hit my head, producing a racquetball-size knot and later a black eye, along with a broken left arm. She invited me to tell her more about the events surrounding this injury. I explained that I had met my birth family a few weeks prior. My plans were to visit them again the day after my accident. I canceled my trip because of the concussion.

She proceeded with her work as I relaxed and fell asleep. The session over, she requested I set another appointment. I agreed. In the week that followed, I had only one incident of blurred vision, which compared favorably to my prior experience of many episodes a day. I was in awe of the precious gift of sight, and promised myself I would never take it for granted again.

Both eager and relaxed I arrived for my next appointment. While I lay on her table, she queried me about my relationship with my birth parents. I explained that I had met them just after my thirty-eighth birthday. They are wonderful, gracious people and had lovingly welcomed me back into their family. I continued to stay in touch with them, visiting them several times a year. *What is happening now?* she inquired. I told her that, in a month, they would be treating the entire family, that is, my family along with my birth brother, sister, in-laws and grandchildren to a cruise.

And how to you feel about that? she asked. *Grateful,* I replied. *And what else?* she inquired. Raised to be cultured and well mannered, I knew I was supposed to be grateful, and I was truly grateful. I did not want to admit to any other feelings. It was not the proper thing to do. *Do you really want to heal your eye?* she questioned. *Well there were these little nagging thoughts,* I replied. *What is true today, is that there is enough money for us all to go on a cruise. Yet there wasn't enough money for me when I was born. I missed thirty-eight years with them. I feel cheated. Looking now it is clear, there was enough money! I have felt a loss my whole life, a missing. I would rather have stayed with them, than be going on this cruise. It seems to high a price to pay, to lose so much time and love, for money.*

As I expressed the myriad of thoughts and feelings buried inside, I felt guilty. I had great parents. They taught me the important things in life and had given me unconditional love. To feel these things seemed to betray them. It also looked like a slap in the face to my birthparents who had taken me into their lives, no questions asked. Yet I as my gut wrenched I could no longer deny the truth, I was angry.

My energy healer stopped me in my tracks. *Don't repress your feelings again and rob yourself of your healing,* she said. *Your feelings are not right or wrong, good or bad, they just are. Accept and appreciate them. Here are your options: call your birthparents and tell them how you feel, or go on the cruise and get deathly ill. You choose!*

Next, fear struck. How could I possibly call these kind people and tell them I was angry? They were in the process of giving me a wonderful gift. And then came the real fear, if I expressed my resentment, they might reject me. That would be unbearable. *Your choice,* she repeated.

Yet fear or not, I knew I had to call. I had to risk to heal. *When are you going to call?* she wondered. *Sunday at seven,* I replied. *Do you want me to call you at six for support, and we will walk through the call?* she asked. *Yes,* I agreed. My course set, I headed back to the office, relieved that Sunday was four days away.

Those four days seemed to pass at the speed of light. Filled with anxiety, I called my energy healer at six on Sunday. She loved me, encouraged me, and we walked through every step of the call. She reassured me it would all turn out well.

At seven I phoned my birthparents. By the time they answered the phone, I was in tears, my voice jagged between sobs. I began, *I need to talk to you. My request is that you listen. My intention is that love be present at the end of this call.* I paused, more sobs, I took a few deep breaths. Then the most beautiful thing occurred. My birthparents said, *You can say anything to us, anything at all, and we will love you. We have always loved you and always will.*

You may change your mind I said, ever skeptical of being loved. Tears flowing I continued, *I am angry that there is enough money for us all to go on a cruise! I missed so many years and it hurts in my heart.* I touched my chest; I could feel the pain. *I would rather have been with you all those years that go on this cruise. I am grateful for the gift, but I am angry and hurt all at the same time.* Now we were all crying. My birthparents repeated, *You can say anything to us, anything at all, and we will love you. We have always loved you and always will.* The pain in my chest began to lessen. Rejection, my worst fear, had not come to pass. In its place I received unconditional love.

More conversation, more tears and our call was complete. Love was present. I was on cloud nine. A passage from the Bible came to me from my childhood, *tho I walk through the valley of the shadow of death, I will fear no evil, for thou art with me.* I was sure I had just walked through a dark foreboding valley, and had emerged into the sun and the presence of Universal love at the other side.

In this frightening, yet simple, conversation I healed on many levels. By releasing my old fear and resentment, I made room for and received unconditional love. My relationship with money was changed forever. I no longer needed to be hostage to the money fantasies that I am not worthy or that there is not enough money.

My left eye never again got the jitters. I went on to use energy healing to repair many other parts of my body. I now engage some kind of bodywork at least bi-weekly. As a physical form, my body can tell me things in a concrete way. It does not lie. I pay attention to my aches and tight spots as messengers to look and see, what else might be there. Then I honor the voice of my body by taking care of it.

I learned another invaluable lesson in this journey. I discovered that when I powerfully take care of myself, life works. Everyone else gets taken care of too. As I healed, my birthparents healed. I had expressed the unspeakable, and in so doing, released it from our relationship so we could grow together in love on a foundation of integrity.

This is Mackey's story. It is shared here for the purpose of our mutual healing. It is her wish that you unearth and release the money fantasies holding you back from your prosperity. In so doing, you provide an opening for your own healing and healing in your communities, be it your home, workplace, church, or with your friends.

We at Prosperity Publishing, LLC honor your path and transformation.
We want to hear from you.

Send us your stories.
stories@prosperitypublishing.com
http://www.prosperitypublishing.com

Joy

Let me tell you who I am
I will not hide
I will not shy away from prominence
I am destined to be big
I came to transform lives
I am joy

Deep joy
   Abiding joy
      Full-hearted joy
         Orgasmic joy
            Joy for the sake of itself

I will be who I came to be
The shame of my past will not stand in my way
I will walk through my fear
Bringing the opportunity created by conscious choice

People are bound by patterns
I unlock them even before they know their own confinement

I bring joy in money
But it really isn't about money
For money is just something human beings made up
We use it in so many ways

To compete
   To control
      To hurt each other
         To have fun
            To worry over

My gift is to stand for your future
Even before you see where you are going, I see
I vision who you will become
You are big
You have much to contribute
I will be there as you leave the boundaries of what you know
and fly away into your abundant future

And I am blessed by your transformation ■

Resources

Resources

THE ENNEAGRAM

International Enneagram Association:
http://www.intl-enneagram-assn.org

Authentic Enneagram:
http://www.authenticenneagram.com

COACHING and NETWORKING

The 5th Field: A prosperity business coaching system.
http://www.the5thfield.com

Conscious Living Center: Deborah Ooten, PhD, Life Coach.
enneagramconnect@aol.com

Michael Gerber: Author of *The E-Myth Revisited.*
http://www.e-myth.com

BNI: A business professional networking organization that offers each member the opportunity to share ideas, contacts and referrals.
http://www.bni.com

Dr. Ivan Misner: Founder and CEO of BNI (Business Network International), founded in 1985. Called the Networking Guru by *Entrepreneur Magazine,* he has been nominated twice for *Inc. Magazine's* Entrepreneur of the Year Award. Dr. Misner is a world-renowned speaker and has written five books, including *Masters of Networking.* See BNI for website.

Flow National: A national association promoting a lifestyle of wholeness expanding mind, body and spirit.
http://www.flownational.com

Jennifer Read Hawthorn: Her success as a trainer and speaker provided the impetus for her latest book, *Chicken Soup for the Mother's Soul.* This book reached #1 on *USA Today's* bestseller list, becoming the first Chicken Soup for the Soul book to achieve that status. The book also made #1 on *Publisher's Weekly* and the *New York Times* bestseller lists.

SPIRITUAL AND PERSONAL GROWTH

Association of Unity Churches:
http://www.unity.org

Edwene Gaines, Unity Minister:
http://www.prosperityproducts.com

Eckhart Tolle: Author of *The Power of Now*, Tolle is a counselor and spiritual teacher, working with individuals and small groups in Europe and North America.
http://www.eckharttolle.com

Soulful Living: Links to various sites including prosperity.
http://www.soulfulliving.com

Carolyn Myss:
http://www.myss.com

Nightingale Conant:
http://www.nightingaleconant.com

Joan Borysenko:
http://www.joanborysenko.com

Stephen Covey:
http://www.franklincovey.com

Anthony Robbins:
http://www.tonyrobbins.com

HOLISTIC HEALING

EMDR: Eye movement desensitization and reprocessing
http://www.emdr.com

The Wellness Institute:
http://www.thewellnessinstitute.net

Auriculotherapy: Also called ear acupuncture, auriculotherapy is being used for pain control and diagnosis of health conditions.
http://www.auriculotherapy-intl.com

Rodale Press:
http://www.rodalepress.com

Holistic Medicine: Articles and websites that focus on holistic healing.
http://www.holisticmed.com

American Yoga Foundation:
http://www.alignment.org

Cranio-Sacral Healing:
http://www.craniosacraltherapy.com

PUBLISHING

Prosperity Publishing: Specializes in topics of interest to women by mostly women authors.
http://www.prosperitypublishing.com

WRITING

Women Writing for (a) Change: Since 1991, a Cincinnati-based writing center offering writing classes, workshops, retreats and a supportive community for women and girls.
http://www.womenwriting.org

GOVERNMENT

Social Security Administration: information about social security benefits.
http://www.ssa.gov

Savings bonds: buying guide for US Savings bonds.
http://www.savingsbond.gov

MEDIA

PBS: PBS, headquartered in Alexandria, Virginia, is a private, non-profit media enterprise owned and operated by the nation's 349 public television stations.
http://www.PBS.org

US News: Comprehensive online news resource.
http://www.usnews.com

I village: Comprehensive women's site.
http://ivillage.com

CNBC: News site.
http://www.cnbc.com

Wisdom Media Group: Internet and cable radio and satellite television station.
http://www.wisdommedia.com

CREDIT COUNSELING

http://www.consumercredit.com

http://www.nfcc.org

http://www.actec.org

LEGAL

Consumer Law Page: Provides practical legal first aid on a variety of consumer and legal issues.
http://www.consumerlawpage.com

Findlaw:
http://www.findlaw.com

ESTATE PLANNING

Estate Planning Links: This site contains hundreds of well-organized, time-saving links to estate planning, elder law, tax and related websites.
http://www.estateplanninglinks.com

National Association of Financial and Estate Planning: One of the articles on this site includes a discussion of the financial and retirement planning aspects of estate planning.
http://www.nafep.com

American College of Trust and Estate Counsel: Association of lawyers skilled in a wide range of legal maatters.
http://www.actec.org

Partnership for Caring: A national nonprofit organization that partners individuals and organizations to improve how people die in our society. (Also called Advance Directives).
http://www.partnershipforcaring.org

COLLEGE PLANNING.

College Planning Service: An independent college consulting company based in Kirkland, Washington, which helps students attend colleges and universities throughout the United States.
http://www.collegeplanning.com
See also: http://www.collegeplanning.org

Financial Aid for College: Free form to apply for financial aid for college.
http://www.fafsa.ed.gov

FINANCE AND INVESTING

Mackey McNeill Mohr PSC:
http://www.mmmpsc.com

Ran One: The world's largest network of independent accounting firms. Operating in the three global regions of the Americas, Europe and Asia-Pacific.
http://www.ranone.com

Bloomberg: Provides combination of data, analytics, electronic trading and straight-through processing tools in a single platform.
http://www.bloomberg.com

Fool: Personal finance, news and investing.
http://www.fool.com

The Street: Stock news, investing basics and personal finance.
http://www.thestreet.com

Certified Financial Planners: Learn about financial planning.
http://www.cfp-board.org

Kiplinger: Personal finance information and business forcasts.
http://www.kiplinger.com

American Association of Individual Investors: Specializes in providing education in the area of stock investing, mutual funds, portfolio management and retirement planning.
http://www.aaii.com

FINANCIAL CALCULATORS

College cost oriented site:
http://www.finaid.org

Mortgage.investing and personal finance site:
http://www.calcbuilder.com

Quicken™: Comprehensive financial site.
http://www.quicken.com

Intelliquote: Compare term life insurance quotes online.
http://www.intelliquote.com

Money Central: MSN site with comprehensive money resources.
http://www.moneycentral.com

SaveWealth: Offers access to a wide range of mutual funds, stocks, timely research, and tax-effective investments.
http://www.savewealth.com

Accuquote: Compare the price, features, and financial strength of over 1,600 life insurance products.
http://www.accuquote.com

Morningstar: Independent help for successful investing.
http://www.morningstar.com

Smart Money: Joint venture company of Dow Jones and Company and Hearst Communications.
http://www.smartmoney.com

Portfolio builder: You can open an account online, decide which securities you want to buy,choose how much money you want to invest into each, and determine how often you want to make your automatic repeat purchases.

http://www.moolera.com

Better Homes and Garden: Families and their money.
http://www.familymoney.com

Bank Rate: Comprehensive money site.
http://www.bankrate.com

Financial designations: Lists designations of financial service professionals.
http://www.financial-designations.8m.com

INSURANCE

Instant Insurance Quotes:
http://www.insure.com

Long Term Care Insurance: Information regarding how to care for health care costs for the elderly.
http://www.longtermcareinsurance.org

SOCIALLLY RESPONSIBLE INVESTING (SRI)

Corporate Register: Provides a list of 600 corporations that issue sustainability reports on how their businesses affect the environment and human rights.
http://www.corporateregister.com

Folio: Helps investors select socially responsible stock for diverse portfolios.
http://www.foliofn.com

Social Funds: Offers social and ethical information about more than 1800 companies.
http://www.socialfunds.com

Social Investing: social, ethical and environmental investing and consumer and corporate accountability.
http://www.goodmoney.com

Social Investing: Socially responsible investing.
http://www.greenmoneyjournal.com

Women Quoted Within This Book

SHIRLEY ABBOTT: Southern writer of social conditions in the rural South.

SUSAN B. ANTHONY: Developed her sense of justice and moral zeal through her upbringing in her Quaker family with long activist traditions. Became active in temperance. Because she was a woman, she was not allowed to speak at temperance rallies. She joined the women's rights movement in 1852.

EVE ARDEN: Television actress and star of *Our Miss Brooks* in the 1950's.

MARY MCLEOD BETHUNE: Champion in the battle for African-American women's rights. She founded Bethune-Cookman College and served as an advisor on African American affairs to four presidents. She was appointed Director of the Division of Negro Affairs of the National Youth Administration by President Roosevelt and was the first African American woman to hold so high an office in the federal government.

MARLENE DIETRICH: An exotic actress of the 1930s and '40s, she performed around the world and recorded for Decca, Columbia and Capitol.

ELLA FITZGERALD: Considered one of the greatest jazz vocal artists who ever lived.

EDWENE GAINES: Owner-director of Rock Ridge Retreat Center in Valley Head, Alabama. An ordained Unity minister for 23 years, she is also president of The Masters' School and has trained over 400 Master Prosperity Teachers. A Certified Firewalking Instructor, she facilitates the Firewalking Ceremony several times each year.

HELEN KELLER: Blind from age 18 months. She waged a slow, hard and successful battle to overcome her blindness, became well educated, and worked tirelessly for the American Foundation for the Blind.

FLORENCE NIGHTINGALE: A legend in her lifetime who was appointed during the Crimean War in 1854 to oversee the introduction of female nurses into the military hospitals in Turkey. Her best-known works were *Notes on Nursing* and writing on public health. She published 200 books, reports and pamphlets. She was awarded the Royal Red Cross in 1883 by Queen Victoria.

ELEANOR ROOSEVELT: A shy and awkward child starved for recognition, she grew up to be a woman with great sensitivity to the underprivileged. Eleanor was the wife of Franklin D. Roosevelt, President of the United States during the Depression. After President Roosevelt's death, she continued her work and became an American spokesperson in the United Nations.

LILLIAN EUGENE SMITH: Established a written legacy that identified and challenged the ways that racism destroys families, communities and the dreams of freedom and democracy.

ELLA WHEELER WILCOX: Began writing poetry at age thirteen. Best known work: *Poems of Passion*.

Appendices

Appendix A

Statement of Financial Position

As of (date) _____

Lifestyle assets:

Personal residence: $_____

Second or vacation home: $_____

Automobiles:

     _____ $_____

     _____ $_____

     _____ $_____

Collectables:

     _____ $_____

     _____ $_____

     _____ $_____

Household:

     _____ $_____

     _____ $_____

     _____ $_____

Other:

     _____ $_____

     _____ $_____

     _____ $_____

Total fair market value of lifestyle assets: $_____

...Statement of financial position

Lifestyle liabilities:

Personal residence mortgage: $_____

Second or vacation home mortgage: $_____

Automobiles loans:

    _____ $_____

    _____ $_____

    _____ $_____

Credit card debt:

    _____ $_____

    _____ $_____

    _____ $_____

Other:

    _____ $_____

    _____ $_____

    _____ $_____

Total obligations of lifestyle liabilities: $_____

Net worth, lifestyle: $_____

(Assets minus liabilities)

...Statement of financial position

Investment assets:

After tax assets:

Checking accounts:

      _____ $_____

      _____ $_____

      _____ $_____

Savings accounts:

      _____ $_____

      _____ $_____

      _____ $_____

Certificates of deposit:

      _____ $_____

      _____ $_____

      _____ $_____

Money market accounts:

      _____ $_____

      _____ $_____

      _____ $_____

Mutual funds:

      _____ $_____

      _____ $_____

      _____ $_____

...Statement of financial position

Individually held stocks or securities:

_____ $_____

_____ $_____

_____ $_____

Individually held bonds:

_____ $_____

_____ $_____

_____ $_____

Brokerage accounts:

_____ $_____

_____ $_____

_____ $_____

Rental real estate:

_____ $_____

_____ $_____

_____ $_____

Business or professional practice:

_____ $_____

_____ $_____

_____ $_____

…Statement of financial position

Other:

       _____ $_____

       _____ $_____

       _____ $_____

Tax-deferred accounts:

IRA:

       _____ $_____

       _____ $_____

       _____ $_____

401(k):

       _____ $_____

       _____ $_____

       _____ $_____

Company-sponsored pension:

       _____ $_____

       _____ $_____

       _____ $_____

Other:

       _____ $_____

       _____ $_____

       _____ $_____

Total investment assets: $_____

...Statement of financial position

Investment liabilities:

Mortgages, rental property:

_____ $_____

_____ $_____

_____ $_____

Margin loans:

_____ $_____

_____ $_____

_____ $_____

Loans to acquire business interests:

_____ $_____

_____ $_____

Other:

_____ $_____

_____ $_____

_____ $_____

Total obligations of investment liabilities: $_____

Net worth, investment: $_____
(Assets minus liabilities)

Total net worth, investment and lifestyle: $_____

Percentage of net worth, lifestyle: _____%

Percentage of net worth, investment: _____%

Appendix B

Cash flow analysis, inflows

Return on labor:

      Gross pay _____ $_____

      Gross pay _____ $_____

      Gross pay _____ $_____

Total return on labor: $_____ ___%

Return on assets:

Stock dividends: $_____

Interest earned: $_____

Closely held business: $_____

      S Corp distributions: $_____

      C Corp dividends: $_____

      Partnership distributions: $_____

Rental property net cash flow: $_____

Royalties: $_____

Dividends and capital gains inside retirement plans: $_____

Other: $_____

Other: $_____

Total return on assets: $_____ ___%

…Cash flow analysis, inflows

Return on combination of assets and labor:

Closely held business:

     S Corp distributions: $_____

     C Corp dividends: $_____

     Partnership distributions: $_____

Rental property net cash flow: $_____

Other: $_____

Other: $_____

Other: $_____

Total mixed return cash flow: $_____ ___%

Gifts:

     Source:

     _____ $_____

     _____ $_____

     _____ $_____

     _____ $_____

     _____ $_____

Total gifts: $_____ ___%

Total inflows, all sources: $_____ ___%

Appendix C

Cash flow analysis, outflows

Use this outline to help you get started. If you are using a computerized program, set up the system using these categories.

Taxes:

Federal income tax:	$_____
State income tax:	$_____
Local income tax:	$_____
Social Security tax:	$_____
Medicare tax:	$_____
Real estate tax:	$_____
Personal property tax:	$_____
Other taxes:	$_____
_____	$_____
_____	$_____

Total taxes: $_____ ____%

Savings, pre-tax: $_____ ____%

Savings, after tax: $_____ ____%

…Cash flow analysis, outflows

Debt payments, principal and interest:

_____ $_____

_____ $_____

_____ $_____

_____ $_____

Total debt payments: $_____ ____%

Insurance:

    Health: $_____

    Life: $_____

    Disability: $_____

    Homeowners: $_____

    Automobile: $_____

    Other: _____ $_____

Total insurance: $_____ ____%

Cost of primary home:

    Utilities: $_____

    Cable TV: $_____

    Telephone: $_____

...Cash flow analysis, outflows

       Repairs and maintenance: $_____

       Improvements: $_____

       Internet service: $_____

       Cleaning: $_____

       Lawn care: $_____

       Furnishings: $_____

       Water and sewer: $_____

       Other: $_____

Total costs of home: $_____ _____%
(excluding mortgage and insurance)

Cost of second home:

       Utilities: $_____

       Cable TV: $_____

       Telephone: $_____

       Repairs and maintenance: $_____

       Improvements: $_____

       Internet service: $_____

       Cleaning: $_____

       Lawn care: $_____

       Furnishings: $_____

       Water and sewer: $_____

       Other: $_____

Total costs of home: $_____ _____%

...Cash flow analysis, outflows

(excluding mortgage and insurance)

Other spending, necessity:

Automobile:

      Gas: $_____

      Repairs: $_____

      Lease: $_____

      Maintenance: $_____

Groceries: $_____

Health care:

      Dental: $_____

      Chiropractic: $_____

      Physician: $_____

      Hospital: $_____

      Pharmacy: $_____

      Therapy: $_____

      Energy work: $_____

      Gym: $_____

      Massage: $_____

Education:

      Tuition: $_____

      Supplies: $_____

      Lectures: $_____

Travel: $_____

...Cash flow analysis, outflows

   Other: $_____

Charitable giving: $_____

Other:

   _____ $_____

   _____ $_____

   _____ $_____

   _____ $_____

Total spending, necessity: $_____ _____%

Other spending, wants:

   Cash, unidentified: $_____

   Clothing: $_____

Travel:

   Airfare: $_____

   Hotel: $_____

   Other: $_____

Personal care:

   Hair care: $_____

   Cosmetics: $_____

   Other:_____ $_____

    _____ $_____

...Cash flow analysis, outflows

Leisure:

Books and magazines:	$_____
Cultural events:	$_____
Sporting events:	$_____
Movies and video rental:	$_____
Concerts:	$_____
Dining out:	$_____
Entertaining:	$_____
Tapes and CDs:	$_____
Toys and Games:	$_____
Sporting goods:	$_____
Other:	$_____
Gifts:	$_____
Other:	
_____	$_____
_____	$_____
_____	$_____
_____	$_____
_____	$_____

Total spending, wants: $_____ _____%

Total spending: $_____ 100%

More about **Mackey** and her companies

Mackey Miriam McNeill

Mackey McNeill began her accounting firm in 1983. Balancing a new baby on one hip and the books on the other, Mackey built her business to become one of the top accounting firms and one of the largest women-owned businesses in Greater Cincinnati.

A native Georgian, Mackey graduated *cum laude* from the University of Georgia with a Bachelor's in Business Administration. A former controller, Mackey has worked twenty-three years in public accounting for and with both regional and national accounting firms, and has developed accounting curriculum for Xavier University, Cincinnati, Ohio. Mackey holds a CPA Certificate in Kentucky and Ohio, and has her Certificate of Educational Achievement from the AICPA in Personal Financial Planning. She is certified as a Personal Financial Specialist (PFS) by the AICPA. Mackey is also a certified Enneagram teacher in the oral tradition.

Professionally, her honors include:

- Northern Kentucky Accounting Executive of the Year
- YWCA Career Woman of Achievement
- Cincinnati Business and Professional Woman of the Year
- Accountant Advocate of the Year by the Kentucky Small Business Administration.

Mackey believes in and devotes a significant amount of her time to community service. She has held active and leadership roles in many business and civic organizations such as:

- Northern Kentucky Chamber of Commerce
- Greater Cincinnati Chamber of Commerce

- American Institute of CPAs; Kentucky Society of CPAs

- Kentucky Small Business Development Center

- Fine Arts Fund

- United Way

- Northern Kentucky League of Women Voters

- New Thought Unity Center.

Mackey's passion is to help people bring personal power to their relationship to money. Wealthy, in debt, or just hanging in there, most people have a relationship of scarcity or fear around money. In her work with individuals and businesses, she has developed techniques to facilitate transforming this relationship to one of joy. These ideas are captured in her book: *The Intersection of Joy and Money*. Mackey uses her experience and knowledge to lead the reader through a journey of self-discovery and self-actualization — a revolutionary way to create prosperity.

Mackey resides in Ft. Mitchell, Kentucky. She enjoys flyfishing, hiking, rowing, dancing and spending time with her friends and family. She attends New Thought Unity Center in Cincinnati, Ohio. Her daughter Sarah is in college at Northern Kentucky University.

In addition to being a frequent lecturer and guest speaker on business and financial topics, Mackey is a partner in Mackey McNeill Mohr, PSC, an accounting and consulting firm; Mohr Financial Services, Inc., a registered investment advisory company; and also owns The 5th Field, a business coaching system. ■

The 5th Field

- Imagine a business created from your essence
- Imagine a business created from your passion
- Imagine a business that is effortless
- Imagine yourself prosperous

This is the possibility of The 5th Field.

How do I create this magical business?

The 5th Field uses a series of strategic processes and systems to design and bring to life a business model that is a limitless expression of you.

The process is to:
- Identify your essence and passion
- Define the vision and mission of the business
- Look at what the business contributes in the world
- Create products and services that maximize the contribution
- Unblock your old money patterns
- Generate a marketing plan
- Generate an action plan
- Design the next expansion

The 5th Field is a transformation process. As a 5th Fielder, your role is one of taking on risk. Trying new things. Constantly removing roadblocks.

Our role is to facilitate the process. We begin by assigning your own personal 5th Field Prosperity Coach. Your Coach tracks the process, keeps the business on track, and defines what is next.

What can you expect from your 5th Field Prosperity Coach?
- To be your ardent cheerleader
- To continually vision your future
- To be non-judgmental about your personal roadblocks
- To be your partner in success
- To act in integrity

So what is in a name?

The 5th Field is the name for the dimension in which the work is done. The first three fields are the three physical dimensions. The 4th field is time. The 5th Field is beyond time and physical dimensions; it is pure creation.

Who can be a 5th Fielder?

Both existing and start-up businesses can be in The 5th Field. The criteria for entrance are:
- A desire to create a business that is a limitless expression of personal essence and passion
- A willingness to take on risk
- An eagerness to let go of your limitations and your past reality around money
- An openness to coaching
- An ability to communicate your needs

The 5th Field is not for everyone. It is limited to fully committed participants.

To find out more about The 5th Field, we suggest you experience it. All participants begin with an initial consultation. We assess where you are and identify the strategic next steps. All you risk in this initial consultation is a look into your future. Your complete satisfaction is required before payment is accepted.

http://www.the5thfield.com

In one week, I deposited more in my bank account than my annual revenue at the time of starting The 5th Field coaching process.

Lucy Morris
Phoenix Possibilities, Inc.

**Mackey McNeill Mohr, PSC
and Mohr Financial Services, Inc.**

Cultivating Client Prosperity

Our vision:

To cultivate client prosperity.

Our mission:

To provide financial services which are comprehensive, value-added and holistic to businesses and individuals. To deliver our services with care and concern. To provide a joyful and engaging environment for our team. To contribute to the forward movement of our community. To live our values.

Four levels of service are offered:

Basic Business Tax and Financial Analysis

Basic service is designed to give you what you need to comply with tax laws and banking arrangements. These services include income tax return preparation, and the assortment of other basic fulfillment matters.

Shared Controller™ and Shared CFO™

Our experienced Shared Controllers and CFOs support you by preparing and overseeing your budget for profit planning purposes, interpreting your financial data and establishing and monitoring key performance indicators. With our assistance, you stay focused and on target with your business plan. This level of service also includes tax planning services designed to give you an immediate return on your investment.

Business Consulting

At this level, we are actively involved with the development and implementation of your strategic plan. Our aim is to make your business more profitable, valuable and enjoyable. We focus on your quality-of-life issues, coupled with implementation of proven, best business practices. These services include business plan development, customer service training, Grow Your Business roundtables, compensation planning, and a variety of other capacity-building services.

Personal Services

Our individual services include both compliance and tailored advisory services. The compliance area includes income tax, gift and information reporting return preparation. Advisory services include comprehensive wealth management as well as tax and financial planning. Investment analysis and management is provided in alignment with your values.

http://www.mmmpsc.com

Order Form

☐   Yes! I want more of Mackey McNeill!

☐   Please contact me with information on having Mackey speak at my next event.

☐   Please contact me about The 5th Field.

☐   Please send *The Intersection of Joy and Money*.

Number of copies _____ @ $24.95   _____

Sales tax 6% (KY residents only)   _____

Shipping & Handling ($5.95 per book)   _____

Total Amount of Order   _____

Name _____

Address _____

City_____State_____Zip _____

Phone _____

Email address _____

☐ Mastercard   ☐ Visa   ☐ American Express   ☐ Discover

Card # _____

Expiration date _____/_____

Or make checks payable to Prosperity Publishing, LLC
and mail or fax to:

Prosperity Publishing, LLC
1881 Dixie Highway, Suite 100
Ft. Wright, KY 41011-2646
(859) 578-4674 • (800) 880-9863 • Fax: (859) 331-4695

To order online: http://www.joyandmoney.com